AUTHOR ROBBINS, L.   Baron Robbins.

TITLE   Higher education revisited.

SUBJECT No.
    378.41

BOOK No.

    253382

P53178-B1(C)

HIGHER EDUCATION REVISITED

Also by Lord Robbins

AGAINST INFLATION
AN ESSAY ON THE NATURE AND SIGNIFICANCE OF
  ECONOMIC SCIENCE
AUTOBIOGRAPHY OF AN ECONOMIST
ECONOMIC CAUSES OF WAR
THE EVOLUTION OF MODERN ECONOMIC THEORY
MONEY, TRADE AND INTERNATIONAL RELATIONS
POLITICAL ECONOMY: PAST AND PRESENT
POLITICS AND ECONOMICS
THE THEORY OF ECONOMIC DEVELOPMENT IN THE
  HISTORY OF ECONOMIC THOUGHT
THE THEORY OF ECONOMIC POLICY IN ENGLISH
  CLASSICAL POLITICAL ECONOMY

HIGHER EDUCATION REVISITED

Lord Robbins

First published 1980 by
THE MACMILLAN PRESS LTD
London and Basingstoke
Associated companies in Delhi
Dublin Hong Kong Johannesburg Lagos
Melbourne New York Singapore Tokyo

Printed in Great Britain by
Billing and Sons Ltd
Guildford, London and Worcester

British Library Cataloguing in Publication Data

Robbins, Lionel, *Baron Robbins*
   Higher education revisited
   1. Education, Higher – Great Britain
   I. Title
   378.41   LA636.8

   ISBN 0–333–28606–5

Contents

Preface

The title of this little book may suggest a systematic treatise. But the introductory chapter gives the reasons why I have cast my reflections on the subjects with which it deals in the essentially informal shape of replies to an imaginary friend. I hope that this will not be thought frivolous. I do, indeed, regard the questions dealt with as being of quite fundamental importance in the sphere to which they belong. But my object here is to state and explain various personal attitudes rather than to provide a comprehensive exposition. Therefore, I have tried to make my presentation as little like an official document as I possibly can.

I will not mention the names of those whom I have consulted in this connection since I know that some of the opinions I have expressed may give offence in some quarters; and I should be reluctant to involve, even indirectly, any person other than myself. But this does not prevent me from expressing gratitude to all who have helped me either by suggestion or criticism.

The London School of Economics   ROBBINS
and Political Science, July 1979

Acknowledgements

I am grateful to the University of Washington Press for permission to use in Chapters 8 and 10 certain paragraphs from a lecture originally delivered at Reed College, Portland, Oregon, and subsequently published in 1970 in a symposium entitled *Individuality and the New Society*, edited by Abraham Kaplan.

1 Introduction

My dear X,

You have asked that I should furnish you with a more or less systematic review of the recommendations and the upshot of the *Committee on Higher Education* of which I was chairman in the early 1960s. And I should be disposed to agree that something on these lines would not be without its uses. An interim survey on certain aspects of developments subsequent to the report of the committee was published in 1969 in the valuable *Impact of Robbins* by Messrs Richard Layard, John King and Claus Moser. But much water has flowed under the bridge since then; and a full and up to date analysis of the matters dealt with by these authors would certainly be illuminating.

But, so far as I am concerned, such an analysis will not be forthcoming. For me the labours I devoted to the work of the committee are now ancient history. I am grateful to have been associated with it and still more grateful for what I learnt during the process from my various colleagues and some of those who gave evidence. As I intimated in my *Autobiography of an Economist*, having regard to the usual fate in recent years of public investigations of this nature, we were lucky – perhaps because a general election was at hand – in having so many of our recommendations accepted; and some at least of the rejections had considerable cogency. But, at my time of life, it would be tedious for me to undertake a point by point review of the conclusions which we reached and the consequences which have followed from their acceptance or rejection; and, since I should be writing against the grain, I think it would be tedious too for you as reader.

But you must not think that since those years I have abandoned interest in problems of higher education. In a more modest way and in spite of many other activities, business and public, I have continued to be an academic – I am happy to say that I am still allowed to lecture two mornings a week for two out of three terms at the London School of Economics. From 1968 to 1974 during a period of considerable anxiety, disciplinary and financial, I was Chairman of the Court of Governors of that institution and am still a member of that body. A much less anxious time, save for one disturbing occurrence and its sad consequence, was when I was Chancellor for ten years from 1968 to 1978 of the University of Stirling, a new foundation recommended by our committee; this is a post which has brought me into contact with all sorts of arrangements with which earlier I had only nodding acquaintance. And speaking in less detail, it would have been unnatural if, having devoted more than three years of my life to intensive study of the wider field, I should have lost interest in the problems which have already emerged and which seem likely to emerge in time to come. On the contrary, they remain for me matters of intense intellectual interest and great importance for our national future.

What I propose, therefore, as an alternative to your suggestion, is that we should exchange letters on these subjects. You shall put questions in whatever order seems to you suitable and I will try to answer them according to my present lights. This will have a double advantage: it will freshen me up to survey these problems in their new aspects; at the same time, by its informality, it will avoid any pretensions to exhaustiveness or over-systemisation. Most modern books on education that I have ever read – and they have been legion – with the exception of Lord Ashby's and one or two others, are very heavy going. It would be my hope that this epistolary method may liven things up a bit and make the subjects we deal with somewhat more acceptable to the general reader.

One further point. My suggestion is that the main focus of our attention shall be the problems of the universities. This is not (repeat *not*) because I think that university affairs are the be-all and end-all of education in general. Perish the thought: only a relatively small proportion of the population go to universities or are suited to go to universities; and the problems of how education in general shall be organised clearly cover a much wider field. Even in the sphere of higher education, the universities are only a part. But for good or for bad – and I don't exclude the latter alternative – in all sorts of ways they tend to have an influence over a much wider area. Moreover, what I know about higher education – and it is still pretty superficial in many respects – centres largely on what takes place in universities. Therefore, although I hope that from time to time we may range over the wider field, I embark on this correspondence with the problems of universities chiefly in mind.

If you agree with all this, it is now up to you to begin the cross-examination.

Yours etc.

2 *Raison d'Etre*

My dear X,

You begin our proposed correspondence with the question what is the use of universities?

There is an ambiguity in this question which must at once be dragged into the open. Either it may mean what do we expect of universities as ideal types – what do we aim at in supporting their existence? Or it may mean what is the actual utility of universities – to what extent do they fulfil or fail to fulfil our expectations and justify our support? The answers to the second of these questions must be very complicated: there are good and bad features of universities as at present constituted. Thus they can only emerge as you pose to me questions on particular aspects of their operation and services. But the question of the ultimate *raison d'être* of universities according to modern expectations is clearly primary as establishing criteria, and thus, although difficult, must be tackled here and now.

If we go back into history we find a series of changing conceptions. There can be no doubt that the main objective of the early universities was training for special vocations, conspicuously the priesthood, the law and medicine. Needless to say, this involved the fostering and preservation of much of what there was of general philosophic culture which had survived the Dark Ages. But the advancement of knowledge as such was certainly not a primary objective of these semi-monastic communities.

It is an interesting circumstance that, as time went on, this vocational function tended, if not actually to recede, to constitute a statical feature of a widening horizon. And while the increased prestige of natural science gradually gave rise to new subjects considered eligible for university study and teaching, it was the alleged value of universities as conveying knowledge of the world and the universe which sustained their respectability. The training aspect was played down; indeed it was only in the last 100 years that technologies other than law and medicine have generally been regarded as suitable university subjects. In central Europe, indeed, where the practical significance of such subjects was earlier recognised than in the United Kingdom, attempts were made to segregate them in technical high schools inferentially lower in the intellectual hierarchy than universities, intentions which in some quarters the march of events has largely frustrated – the Technical High School of Zurich, for instance, has an intellectual standing that is probably superior to the various traditional universities of Switzerland.

Thus, until comparatively recent times, the development of universities, outside the exceptions which provided the pretext for their birth, tended much more to be justified in terms of the provision of what was called a liberal education than in terms of training for future careers; and for a very long time in most places the term liberal education consisted in what would now be regarded as a quite disproportionate extent to the ancient languages and their literature whose direct connection with the subsequent activities of the students was, to say the least, very tenuous. But although some of this was done very badly, as can be gathered from the testimony of Adam Smith, Gibbon and Bentham regarding the condition of Oxford in the eighteenth century, it would be wrong to refuse the claims of liberal education as an enlargement of the general powers of the mind to be classified as, both then and now, in the wider sense of the word, training. Many as may be the other attractions of university life – social associations likely to be fruitful later on, sport and various forms of culture, not to mention the intrinsic enjoyment of the acquisition and pursuit of knowledge, it is certainly doubtful if universities would have proved as attractive as they have been, if the belief were not widely held that the courses pursued would not be, directly or indirectly, of some advantage in subsequent careers.

Side by side, however, with the discharge of the function of training the young, there has developed, especially in recent times the function of the preservation and advancement of knowledge. In the beginning the emphasis was on preservation and doubtless this may have involved some obstruction to advancement. To retain historical perspective, it must never be forgotten how much of scholarship and scientific discovery took place outside the universities of Europe. It was not the universities which fostered the work of Spinosa or Hume, nor that of Faraday or Darwin. Nevertheless, from the Renaissance onwards, a substantial proportion of contributions of this sort was produced by those who at some time or other held teaching positions in universities – the names of Newton, Bentley and Adam Smith spring at once to mind – and in modern times the explicit recognition of this function has become more and more widespread. It is arguable indeed that, in some quarters at the present day, the emphasis on the necessity of research on the part of all teachers is to some extent at the expense of their duties in regard to their students. Be this as it may, possibly to be discussed later between us, it will be commonly admitted that nowadays our expectations of universities are at least twofold: they must provide training and they must foster the preservation and advancement of knowledge. On this general conception two elucidations will not be out of order.

The first has regard to the nature of training. As I have hinted already, despite the avowedly vocational intentions of the foundation of the earlier universities, there developed for a time a pronounced bias against further direct professional or technological orientation. In his *Technology and the Universities* Lord Ashby has provided a classic account of the struggle to establish themselves as recognised subjects of vividly interesting disciplines of this sort; and it is common knowledge that in some not neglible quarters there is still a tendency to look down the nose at such alleged intrusions to the traditional coverage of university institutions. To my way of thinking, this attitude is a reflection on those who maintain it rather than on the subjects in question. The ultimate test for any sort of university training is not whether it fits into this or that arbitrary classification but rather *whether it can be taught so as to enlarge the general powers of the mind*. And I am inclined to think that some of the traditionally 'pure' subjects as historically, and even sometimes contemporaneously, taught, would fail to satisfy that criterion.

The second elucidation concerns the alliance of training with the advancement of knowledge. There is indeed no contradiction in this alliance. The acquisition of knowledge in the wide sense of education to enlarge the powers of the mind fades imperceptibly into its advancement – learning at the undergraduate level becomes research at the graduate level. But separation is conceivable. There is indeed a school of thought which recommends its practice. In the USSR, for instance, the universities are largely confined to teaching; research tends principally to be carried on in separate institutes; and since the organisation of teaching and research involves somewhat different problems, it is not difficult to see some administrative advantages in the separation.

But in my judgement the academic arguments tilt the balance in the opposite direction. I do not doubt that a university whose activities are chiefly confined to passing on an existing tradition of knowledge runs the danger of stereotyped methods and thought. And although the division of labour and resources involved by the combination of teaching and research carries with it difficulties and dangers which are absent where separation exists, it is surely good for the general atmosphere that this should take place. It is good that some at least of those who are eminent in research should from time to time explain the fundamentals of their subject to beginners – it helps them to keep an eye on the broad horizons. And it is good too for the students, even though their immediate object is the assimilation of existing knowledge and techniques, to conduct their studies under the same roof, so to speak, and in personal contact with those who are working at the frontiers. There are quite acute problems here which may crop up in our future exchanges. But in spite of these, for me at least, in most cases the advantage lies in combination rather than divorce.

Training, in the wide sense, research and scholarship – these are the tangible functions we look for in our universities. But there are further matters of ethos, much more difficult to define precisely, but nevertheless legitimate to expect, even if by no means always fulfilled. Certainly I should fail to describe my own feelings about the potentialities of universities in the modern world if I did not make some effort to describe them.

Let me say first what I reject. When I first considered your question, I took down Newman's *Idea of a University*; read by me long ago but largely forgotten. Needless to say, as always, I was enchanted by his marvellous prose and fascinated by his palpable sincerity and dedication. But the positive reaction stopped there. I don't in the least object to provision for the study of theology in universities. But I certainly don't think that a university is incomplete without it or that other branches of study necessarily suffer from its absence. I am not out of sympathy with the value which Newman attaches to knowledge as such – quite the contrary so far as I am personally concerned. But I find entirely unworldly and unhistorical the idea of a university devoted entirely to such ends, regardless of training for subsequent careers or the utility which comes from knowledge. Confucious may have been wrong in his belief in his *Analects* that it would be hard to find a man who had studied for three years without aiming at pay: those of us who have

coordinated research produces tangible benefits to society in general?

Well, you know that in one way or another I have been connected with universities myself. I have never been paid to make such claims as I have mentioned, but there must be some residual bias in my attitude. At the end of one's life one is loath to admit that most of one's activities have been negatively productive. And I must admit that some at least of the cruder claims have, to my understanding, a strong element of the bogus. I simply cannot take seriously any attempt to trace any obvious correlation between rates of growth of gross national product – however this nebulous quantity is measured – and the proportion of the relevant age-groups receiving higher education. Needless to say there must be some correlation between the proportion of highly trained engineers and the prevalence of successful industry attending their operations. It would not be absurd to attempt to establish some connection between the proportion of competently educated doctors and the improvement of health. But I should be greatly surprised if, outside specific vocational correlations of this sort, anything much wider and as tangible could be found; the variables are so numerous and the connections are often so indirect. The law for instance is a highly respectable profession. But who is to say what is cause and what is effect in the relations between gross national product and the proportion of trained barristers and solicitors. There are indeed such considerable variations, both in time and place, between the effectiveness of the organisation of higher education that mere quantitative comparisons must be open to considerable question. Moreover the causes of variation in productivity are themselves so various that any attempt to isolate the influence through time of any one factor must be the subject of serious doubt. And considerations of this sort apply *mutatis mutandis* to scholarship and research. Many sophisticated investigations have been directed to the establishment of tangible connections of the kind I have been discussing. But I must confess that, interesting as they may be, in the outcome they leave me completely unconvinced; and I would regard their use in discussions of public policy regarding higher education in general as specious.

Nevertheless on more general grounds I do hold to the view that institutions of higher education which fulfil the expectations I have indicated do serve a beneficial social function. Doubtless there are questions of cost which have to be weighed at various stages against the benefits accruing. But it cannot be a disadvantage to have a higher proportion of the population whose powers of understanding and exposition have been stretched by suitable systematic teaching beyond the school-leaving age. I shall never forget a remark made to me by R. H. Tawney, who in such matters might have been expected to be somewhat choosy, that he thought 'it difficult to exaggerate the extent to which the United States had benefited by the fact that such a substantial proportion of its citizens had had at least the *smell* of a university.' And I adhere to the arguments already developed that such training is most suitably carried out in establishments where the advancement of knowledge by way of cultivation of scholarships and of scientific speculation is carried on side by side.

But does existing practice in these respects fulfil these expectations? This raises a host of questions which must be the subject of further correspondence.

Yours etc.

3 Content and Specialisation

My dear X,

You reproach me that, in my last letter, I tended to assume that the content of what is studied in universities at the present day could be taken for granted in any discussion of the use of such institutions. I am not sure that I should assume a white sheet in this connection. After all I did expatiate to some extent about the gradual extension of coverage from the original nucleus to the eventual admission, not only of natural science but also of many branches of technology. But I admit that I did not discuss the scope of present-day prescriptions as regards curricula eventhough it is, in my judgement, a very fundamental matter, particularly in this country. I think it would be desirable that I should devote the whole of this letter to it.

The problem relates essentially to the coverage of the studies of individual students. No one nowadays would claim that this should be coterminous with the coverage of the university; whatever may have been the justification for the programmes of the medieval universities, at the present time it would be physically and intellectually impossible for any one student to take all the various courses studied. But the important question still remains to what extent should there be specialisation and at what stages; on this question practice varies widely in different parts of the world and there is no consensus of opinion, particularly in this country concerning what is desirable. There are those who argue that in the modern world the stage at which specialisation should begin must precede admission to the university, indeed that it should begin at later stages in the schools; and there are those who argue the opposite position that the true home of specialisation is in the graduate school when the first degree has been taken. And, needless to say, there are many intermediate positions.

Let me stand back from the picture some way and pose the problem in its broadest perspective.

The classic argument for the advantages of specialisation in general is to be found in the first chapter of Adam Smith's *Wealth of*

Nations. Who can forget his vivid demonstration of the advantages of division of labour whereby the position of the common workman in an advanced society had been raised from that of primitive conditions so that while

> compared indeed with the more extravagant luxury of the great his accommodation must no doubt appear extremely simple and easy; and yet it may be true, perhaps, that the accommodation of an European prince does not so much exceed that of an industrious and frugal peasant as the accommodation of the latter exceeds that of many an African King, the absolute master of the lives and liberties of ten thousand naked savages.[1]

This passage is reasonably well known as are the illustrations accompanying it. What is not so well known, however, is the same author's discussion of the disadvantages of the same division of labour.

'In the progress of the division of labour', he said, 'the employment of the far greater part of those who live by labour, that is, of the great body of the people, comes to be confined to a few very simple operations; frequently to one or two. But the understandings of the greater part of men are necessarily formed by their ordinary employments. The man whose whole life is spent in performing a few simple operations, of which the effects too are, perhaps, always the same or very nearly the same, has no occasion to exert his understanding, or to exercise his invention in finding out expedients for removing difficulties which never occur. He naturally loses, therefore, the habit of such exertion, and generally becomes as stupid and ignorant as it is possible for a human creature to become. The torpor of his mind renders him, not only incapable of relishing or bearing a part in any rational conversation, but of conceiving any generous, noble, or tender sentiment, and consequently of forming any just judgement concerning many even of his ordinary duties of private life. Of the great and extensive interests of his country he is altogether incapable of judging; and unless very particular pains have been taken to render him otherwise, he is equally incapable of defending his country in war. The uniformity of his stationary life naturally corrupts the courage of his mind, and makes him regard with abhorrence the irregular, uncertain and adventurous life of a

1. Op. cit. (Glasgow Edition: Oxford University Press, 1976) pp. 23, 25.

soldier. It corrupts even the activity of his body, and renders him incapable of exerting his strength with vigour and perseverance, in any other employment than that to which he has been bred. His dexterity at his own particular trade seems, in this manner, to be acquired at the expense of his intellectual, social and martial virtues.'[2]

As readers of the *Wealth of Nations* will remember, in order to remedy these tendencies Adam Smith favoured a deliberate educational policy on the part of the sovereign – the provision of small parish schools where more broadening influences might be brought into play – instruction in reading and 'the elementary parts of geometry and mechanics.' He thought that perhaps this might be encouraged by small premiums and badges of distinction and enforced by requiring a certificate of competence in these 'most essential parts of education' before giving permission to enter corporations as freeman or set up in trade either in a village or a town corporate.

Now I would like to suggest that in regard to education itself we are confronted with a somewhat analogous problem involving somewhat analogous remedies. That specialisation is eventually necessary, both for vocational reasons and for the advancement of knowledge, is something which should go without saying; and if I say it now and say it emphatically, it is only in order to avoid all possible misunderstandings on this score. Educational specialisation is necessary in order that there may be available the skills necessary for carrying on the business of an advanced community. It is necessary in order to maintain the highest standards of excellence in various branches of scholarship. It is necessary – or usually necessary – in order to promote intellectual and practical discovery: the graduate schools and research institutes of our age are a tribute to this necessity. There have been some universal geniuses in the past, Leonardo for instance, and there may, conceivably, be some in the future. But the main outstanding contributions to culture and civilisation, in the arts, the humanities or the sciences, have come from men who were specialists.

But specialisation without a broad basis of foundation knowledge has also profound disadvantages. It narrows the windows of the mind. It limits the range of sympathy. It increases mutual dependence but it inhibits mutual understanding. For reasons

2. Ibid., vol. II, pp. 781–2.

which I do not understand, Lord Snow's warnings of the dangers of the separation of cultures not infrequently arouse anger. But I am sure that these dangers are real: and I am sure that they are due, not to some unavoidable tendency in advanced societies practising division of intellectual labour, but rather to that practice unaccompanied by corrective educational influences at an appropriate stage.

Apart from these, there are other disadvantages. It is true that modern economic and political organisation needs high specialisation. But it also needs versatility. It needs potential mobility, the ability to move round without undue pains of adaptation. Nowadays the pace of change is such that, at certain levels, not only the individual may be at a disadvantage if he has but one specialised skill; there is also a disadvantage to society as a whole in that changing conditions of demand cannot so easily be met. The main work of the world is not all done by the highest grade specialists, valuable, nay essential, though these may be: it is done at lower levels where, though some degree of specialisation is desirable, a considerable degree of adaptability is also a desideratum.

Hence surely we have to pursue a double objective in educational policy. While recognising the ultimate necessity of special skills, we must also recognise the desirability of broad foundations and, in the early and middle stages at least, a considerable diversity of fundamental techniques and range of information. The great problem is how to shape our educational structure and methods so as to realise both these aims.

It is sometimes urged, however, that this is unnecessary. What is needed in education, it is argued, is not information but training; and this can be provided as well in one restricted field as in a series of different areas. Indeed it is sometimes contended that it can be better provided, since the restriction of the field permits a thoroughness which in the nature of things is not to be achieved in a wider context; and thoroughness it is said – and said rightly – is one of the principal academic virtues. Such apologia are sometimes applied, not only to defend concentration on one general subject but even concentration within that subject. I have heard it argued, for instance, that all the educational value that can accrue from the study of history can be gained even better from the intensive study of one short period in the history of one country than from any course of wider context.

I find all this very implausible and indeed in some of its

manifestations, truly absurd. It is quite true that there is a considerable number of subjects, the intensive study of any one of which is an excellent training for the mind – I hope we have all outgrown the belief that such training is only to be gained from a study of the ancient languages, valuable though that may be. But it is not true that any one subject provides an adequate background for its own study, let alone for a general educated outlook. We may admit that the criteria of truth are universal and that their application may be learnt in a variety of contexts. But knowledge itself is various and is not to be reduced to a common monad. And although ordinary men and women, as distinct from universal geniuses, cannot take all knowledge for their province, their equipment is singularly inadequate if they have competence in only a narrow branch thereof. Competence in mathematics is not the same as competence in languages; and neither group of disciplines affords even a minimum knowledge of history or natural science. The conception of education as consisting only of training is false, certainly as false as the antithetical conception of education as the mere acquisition of information. And I would go further and say that the belief that the mind can be adequately trained in exercises in only one discipline is also misconceived. The ingredients of the world are very varied; we need to apply the powers of the mind in more than one direction, and on more than one type of material, if their potentialities are to be fully realised. The problem of education is not only a problem of depth, it is also a problem of breadth.

The appropriate combination of these desiderata will, however, vary at different stages. What is appropriate at various stages in schools will not necessarily be appropriate at various stages in universities; and it is in this connection that differences of opinion arise. Few will argue for total specialisation from the very beginning. Few will argue against specialisation at any stage. It is in regard to the mixture at different stages that traditions differ and controversy is intense.

So far as schools are concerned I am unashamedly opposed to specialisation of the kind which has become the prevalent fashion, at least in boys' schools South of the Border. I fully recognise the extent to which current sixth form programmes are influenced by university requirements; and I count it as one of the great disservices to education of many universities that that should be so. Yet it is impossible not to be aware of a school of thought which regards with positive approbation a state of affairs in which lads of fourteen or fifteen are sorted out into science or arts streams and thereafter are acquainted with the intellectual content of the other stream only by way of occasional courses not the subject of examination. I confess I regard this with dismay. In 1960–1, of the school leavers in England and Wales with two or more passes at Advanced level, only 6 per cent had at least one arts subject and one science subject, all the remaining 94 per cent were wholly specialised in arts or science courses only. This seems to me to be little short of a national disgrace; and I venture to suggest that there is no other leading country where such a situation would be possible. In France, in Germany, in the United States, most students pursue broad courses embracing both groups of subjects right up to the school leaving age; and I would certainly argue that the onus of proof that the English system does not represent a damaging and, I would even say, a horrible narrowing at a premature age, rests heavily with those who support it.

It is sometimes argued – considering the eminence of the authorship I say it with grief – it is argued in the Crowther Report, that specialisation at this tender age corresponds to some deep-seated need of adolescence – 'subject-mindedness' I believe is the appropriate jargon. The all-out academic commitment of the boy from fourteen to eighteen, it is argued, is best captured by the opportunity of concentrating on one area of supreme interest. Later on there may come a potential broadening when the mind is once more ready to rove more variously.

I do not know whether this is good psychology, though I must say it certainly does not coincide with the recollections of my own boyhood. But I do submit that it misconceives the central function of education at this stage. We may admit that few adolescents find all subjects equally attractive; it may well be that some at least would prefer to devote their energies only to those which they find most interesting. But that is neither here nor there. The purpose of education at this stage surely is to provide an equipment for communication and understanding. And, for this, the study of no one subject or group of associated subjects is adequate. The educated citizen of the modern age needs some knowledge both of mathematics and natural science on the one side and arts subjects, including languages, on the other; and it is really not a bad thing if, in these formative years, he is obliged to learn how to bend his attention to some subjects which do not at once arouse spontaneous enjoyment. He will not be able to comprehend the world about him if he has devoted the best years of his adolescence to the nearly exclusive study of the one or the other; still more if – which happens, alas, with ever greater frequency South of the Border – he has wasted the time which might have been spent acquiring these essential fundamental techniques in concentration on economics, political science and such like disciplines – subjects for grown-ups *par excellence* which, in my judgement, were better *completely excluded* from the main school curriculum, whatever is done on the side by way of description of familiar civic institutions and current events. It is a depressing experience for a university teacher, as I have been for over 50 years, to be confronted with classes, brought up on myopic specialisation, whose members wilt with anxiety at recourse to elementary algebra or geometry, or giggle at the futility of the recommendation if they are referred to any standard work in French or German. In my humble opinion, in spite of the dedicated idealism which has been associated with sixth form specialisation, it runs the acute danger of becoming an active agent in the disintegration of our common culture. A heavy responsibility rests upon those universities whose entrance requirements encourage or even countenance this tendency.

When we leave the schools for the universities, the situation becomes more complicated. There can be no doubt that specialisation is completely appropriate at the graduate level. Indeed, in our century it is here that the advancement of learning, one of the primary duties of the universities, is most to be expected. The great graduate schools of the United States set – and enforce – standards which have few parallels in any earlier age: and I have no doubt that, if here in this island we are to achieve like excellence in specialist training and facilities for research, a considerable development on such lines is desirable. There are indeed departments and centres of research here which need fear no comparison with elsewhere. But the role of the graduate school in university education is still apt to be underrated on both sides of the Border. There is still too much of the belief that a good honours degree takes a man to the very frontiers of knowledge; and this of course is simply not true.

It is in regard to first degree courses that the position is less clear cut. Let me say at once that I am very far from maintaining that at this stage all specialisation is harmful. Indeed I would agree that even in the most general curriculum some degree of specialisation is inevitable and indeed desirable. The question is how much and when; and, given the variety of subjects and the variety of talents to be catered for, I do not think that any simple formula will cover all possible cases.

Taking a very broad view, I think it is clear that much depends on what happens in the schools. It is obvious that a young man who has had a decently broad education up to the school leaving age can specialise at the university with much less danger to his intellectual and general outlook than one who has not had this advantage. Therefore teachers who set great store by specialisation at the first degree stage, should logically be foremost in insisting on its absence in the years at school, though too often they insist on its presence. If they argue that the 'requisite standard' – whatever that means – cannot be reached at graduation without a good deal of specialisation in the sixth form, then they should politely be told to lower their standards for the first degree and arrange for a higher proportion of the students to go forward to post-graduate training of some sort or another.

But leaving all that on one side, I am very willing to admit that, in some subjects or small groups of subjects, for certain types of mind, a substantial measure of study in depth at the undergraduate stage yields results which are educationally valuable. Most of my life I have done a good deal of teaching in honours schools where the stipulated course has varied at different times in its width and depth of coverage; and though I myself have tended to prefer the periods with a greater degree of breadth, I should be sorry to think that all the effort at other times was wasted. For reasons which will become manifest in a moment, I deplore the narrowness of many honours courses in the universities South of the Border. But I think it would be quite absurd to deny that for some types of students and for some types of future careers they can be educationally valuable.

But this is not true, I am fairly sure, for all types of students and for all types of future careers. The honours specialisation characteristic of most, though not all, English, as distinct from Scottish, universities is at its most suitable for future university teachers or future high experts on the more technical side. In this context, even if, from time to time, it tends to turn out one-sided and one-eyed monsters, there can be no doubt that it has also produced generations of good minds and good scholars who in their day have contributed to the advancement of learning, the enrichment of culture and specialised types of professional knowledge. It would spoil a good case to call this in question.

But not all university students are destined to be dons or high experts. And for those who are not, it is at least doubtful whether first degree courses shaped with the requirements of these very special careers in mind, are necessarily the most useful or spiritually worthwhile. Not all the types of careers in which we should wish to see university trained people engaged, are best served by minds trained chiefly in depth in single subjects. Take, for instance, school-teaching outside the sixth form. Is it so certain that a young man with, shall we say, a lower second in honours economics, as it is all too often taught now, to the neglect of other subjects essential to the understanding of society, is likely to be as useful as one with a middle rating in a broader degree with, shall we say, history, geography and a language. Or, going outside academic careers, are we really prepared to say that one who is going into some general administrative job in business, will be better equipped for the performance of his duties and for the understanding and enjoyment of life, with an intensive study of seventeenth century history of the kind we would get in an honours department in English universities, than many with the more miscellaneous groups they would take in a good Canadian or United States university? I, personally, have little doubt of the answer.

Considerations of this sort have always been relevant to university policy since such policy became conscious of needs beyond training for the law and the priesthood. But today, as I see things, they are even more relevant. In this age in which it has been decided that university education shall be provided for widening numbers of the relevant age-groups, it must be realised that the proportion of those admitted who are likely to become dons or high experts is becoming less and less and the proportion of those who proceed to less specialised functions more and more. If this is so, then surely it is important that our first degree courses should be arranged so as to meet the requirements of the latter – the requirements of the many who do the ordinary work of the world – at least equally with those of the few who are privileged to pursue rarer tasks.

Indeed, I would go further. Without wishing completely to throw overboard, where they prevail, the traditions of more specialised first degrees, I would recommend to those responsible the virtues of greater width, even for those who are destined ultimately to become high specialists. For many years I was actively engaged in graduate teaching at LSE, where, in the past, the graduate school has been recruited as much from abroad as from home. And comparing the recruits with first class honours in specialist degrees from English universities with those from university systems elsewhere with first degrees with a broader basis, it was my impression, year after year, that while, at the beginning, the English 'firsts' were perhaps six or nine months ahead of their broader based fellows from elsewhere, it was surprising how quickly the latter were able to catch up and bring to the business, both of further training and of research, a more catholic and flexible outlook than their initially better technically qualified companions. Even in the concentrated work of the graduate school, there really is some advantage in a broad basis of general education. And I would say that this applies to teachers as well – apart from supreme geniuses.

It is in this connection that I have so great an admiration for the central tradition of the Scottish universities in regard to first degrees. It may well be that the detail and arrangement of the courses is still susceptible of improvement here and there – few human arrangements are not. But the broad principles of wide coverage and absence of premature specialisation seem to me to provide a general basis for university training in modern communities which, in many respects, is vastly superior to the specialisation of many honours degrees South of the Border. And I would add that fewer students arrive at the threshold having been spoilt by premature narrowing of their outlook in sixth forms. I think it is no accident that in the newer parts of the English speaking world, in Canada, in the USA, in South Africa, in Australia and New Zealand, it has usually been the Scottish rather than the English tradition which originally furnished the model for the general conception of undergraduate studies. And, looking to the future and comparing the problems North and South of the border, I would say that the difficulties of the former are slight compared with those of the latter. For in Scotland at most what is needed is experimentation with new combinations and groupings in the first degrees and development of graduate specialisation later on, comparatively straightforward tasks which work – or should work – with the grain of academic inclinations. But in England it is often a problem of a positive reversal of tendencies of developing more generality in first degrees and transferring a good deal of specialisation to a later stage, unwinding so to speak, at both ends – a difficult business likely to be beset with determined resistance from many entrenched academic interests. Therefore whatever innovations they make in future, I profoundly hope that the Scottish universities will never abandon the salutory practice of a broad-based first degree. And so I could go on. In my opinion prevalent thinking on these matters in England has got itself into a thorough mess. It is quite absurd that young persons at the tender age of fourteen or fifteen should be asked to choose whether they want to be humanists or scientists – or much worse still 'social scientists'. And it is equally absurd that so large a proportion of the enlarged university population should be taking highly specialised first degree courses, only directly suitable for future careers as university teachers or branches of extreme expertise. Too many English professors seem to assume that the only way to reputation is to have a flourishing honours undergraduate department, ruining school education in its later stages and neglecting the very considerable number of students who would do better with broader degrees. Educationalists who boast that the English system is the best in the world in this respect must be either very innocent or very insular. Other areas including, thank heaven, Scotland, must, in their judgement, be all out of step.

Yours etc.

4 Numbers and Selectivity

My dear X,

Your comment on my last letter brings me down to realities as distinct from aims and aspirations. You ask what was the justification for the recommendation of the Committee on Higher Education of 1963 that places should be available for all who have the ability and willingness to benefit from them – a recommendation which was at once accepted both by the government of the day and the opposition parties and whose execution has undoubtedly involved a substantial increase of numbers in this educational area.

Let me say at once that this recommendation was accompanied by a condition which is very seldom quoted, although, from my point of view – and the point of view of the committee – it was quite fundamental: the condition, namely, that the expansion should involve a much greater provision of broader courses. We devoted part of a chapter to our reasons for this view and it figures duly in our summary of conclusions. In my last letter I have emphasised my belief that this condition does not prevail in most universities south of the border, which, if correct, certainly means that *an essential condition of this major recommendation has not been fulfilled*. In this letter, however, I shall discuss the general reasons which, *on the assumption that it would be so fulfilled*, led to our recommendation of increased numbers and the problems of selection that it involves.

The broad ground on which these recommendations were based was that there was in prospect a quite definite increase in the number of applications for places – an increase, be it noted, on qualifications which in the past would have been held to be sufficient grounds for admission. If, therefore, additional places were not made available, it followed inevitably that some of such applications which in the past would have been granted, would have had to have been refused; that is to say that admission standards would have had to be raised. *Young people who at earlier times would have been admitted, would have been excluded.*

23

or tests available to enable one to predict with certainty the potentialities of all applicants. Clearly there is a large band where the evidence of present ability is unmistakable – whatever may be its evolution in the future. But the cases at the margin, what honest interviewer can put his hand on his heart and say that he has never made a mistake in this region? Moreover, although there may be failures which are obviously below rigidly drawn lines as regards present performance, who is to say what are the potentialities? Intelligence tests may be alright for gauging specific capacities – quickness of response to the requirements of aviation for instance. But as regards general intelligence I regard them as largely, if not entirely, bogus. How often were we told in my young days that there was no such thing as late development – modern psychology could discover all potentialities at the tender age of five years; and how often as teachers we have found brilliant youngsters who fizzled out and others, with no better than average I.Q.s or worse, turn out to be quite remarkable. Even where it is a question of *précis* or simple mathematics – capacities which it is much more reasonable to demand of applicants for many subjects than stop-watch tests, which incidentally may be trained for, there may easily be problems of nervous tension or dyslexia which even the most sympathetic marking or *viva* cannot circumnavigate. In my judgement the case for some relaxation of present standards is quite considerable.

One method of relaxation would be to accept school leaving certificates at a level somewhat lower than the present requirements of A levels of some arbitrary grade, and to make the final judgement as to who is to be allowed to continue at the end of a year's work. This is already practised in some universities abroad; and it certainly has the merit of permitting greater thoroughness of assessment than anything based on A levels, special examinations and *ad hoc* interviews. There is something wrong with the organisation of teaching, if after a year in an institution of higher education, the future potentialities of a young person cannot be better assessed than at application for admission. I say better, not finally assessed; for some development may be delayed until much later on. I personally have made, or nearly made, mistakes regarding admission even at the graduate school level; and I should be sceptical of any very ambitious claim always to be able to spot talent at any stage whatever. The one year delay in assessing suitability to go on to a full course must always be regarded as a *pis aller*.

But is it generally desirable? I see immense reluctance on the part of some teachers for the extra work involved – motives with which I confess I have not excessive sympathy. But, as regards its acceptability to young people and their parents, I suspect there must be differences according to local expectations and traditions. There are some parts of the world, parts of the United States for instance, where it seems to go down pretty well – presumably on the maxim that it is better to have loved and lost than never to have loved at all. But there are other parts of continental Europe, for instance, where parental expectations and student attitudes are such that the possible disgrace of not being allowed to continue would much more than offset the increase of opportunity of showing one's merit. This might be minimised if shortened pass degrees or diplomas were not viewed with such ridiculous distaste by the majority of teachers. But this is a highly controversial subject.

At this stage in the context of numbers and selection, it is probably desirable to say a few words about a policy which is the exact reverse of the principles underlying the policies recommended by the Committee on Higher Education. This is the so-called policy of educational planning, according to which the government of the day makes estimates of the various types of skill required in the economy and then, having regard to the order achieved in the various preliminary tests, admits to the relevant disciplines the requisite numbers involved. This roughly speaking is the system in vogue in the Soviet Union; and although I have heard of at least one humane exception, I believe it is administered with considerable rigidity. It has also been discussed in some quarters in the free societies of the western world without, I am bound to say, much indication of its implications for an economy which was not totally planned.

Now of course where the government is the employer, as in state schools or the Health Service, it is certainly desirable that it should make estimates of its future requirements as regards different kinds of man or woman power. The task is not without its difficulties: it has to take into account the prices which it will be possible and expedient to pay in these various categories including, of course, the fringe benefits – pension privileges – and the existence of competing alternatives, not to mention the possibility, certainly not excluded in a volatile democracy, that its policies may change halfway through the projected process. It is not an over-statement to say that, hitherto, planning in such connections has not been conspicuously successful. Witness the lamentable position of the present population of the colleges of education. But that is not to deny that it should be attempted.

But it is one thing to make forecasts of the number of teachers of chemistry required in state schools, say, eight years hence. It is quite another thing to plan higher education in general on such lines. It is another thing from the purely technical point of view; and it is another thing from the point of view of the liberty of the individual. Let me be a little more precise on this issue; for in the last analysis both of the way the economy works and of the way it is desirable that it should work, very fundamental differences of outlook are involved.

On the plane of the mechanics of overall planning of this sort and its consequences, there are at least two formidable difficulties. The first is that the demand for skills, like the demands for anything else, depends to some extent on considerations of price. If the price is high relative to available substitutes, then the demand is lower than would otherwise be the case. If it is low, then the consequence is the reverse. I would certainly not wish to be thought to deny the possibility of *any* forecasting in this respect. But I would indeed claim that, in contemporary discussions of general higher education planning, any reference to future relative prices involved is mainly conspicuous by its absence. And if the attempt is made, then having regard to the interdependence of prices, demand and supply in a great many sectors of the market, any definite forecast in one part of the field is likely to be found at best – which is certainly not guaranteed – to be little more than a guess.

There is a further difficulty in this connection which deserves to be dragged into the open, the difficulty, namely, of forecasting the development of technology and its influence on future markets. Formally speaking of course, the general allusion to the interdependence of markets already made could be held to cover this complication. But because of its immense practical importance it deserves separate emphasis. Who can foretell the future of discovery? It is no play on words but rather an essential condition of the world we live in, that if inventions and autonomous changes in technology could be foretold, they would not be *discovery*. Who, 25 years ago could have foretold the immense changes in the organisation of administration and industrial production that are being produced by the spread of computers and computational methods. Even the experts of the Gosplan admitted to me that many of their plans had been falsified by developments in electronics; and one has only to look at the predictions of western 'experts' over the last 50 years regarding the probable development of demand for various kinds of investment, to realise that any precise planning of the production of various kinds of particular skills must be regarded as hazardous in the extreme. Indeed if there is any lesson to be learned from the experience of history in this respect, it is the need which I emphasised in my last letter, for education which is conducive to versatility rather than highly specialised skills liable to be superseded by the unknown.

Apart from these technical difficulties, however, which you must admit are very formidable, there is a further reason for rejecting the project of general educational planning on these lines: the reason namely that it necessarily involves fundamental limitations of human freedom. It involves limitations of choice of education. It involves authoritarian direction of labour. It is difficult to see how it could ever be attempted in any comprehensive form save in a completely totalitarian society. Since this must be a matter of concern to all friends of the free society, perhaps you will bear with me if I develop these points a little further.

Take first limitations of choice. Suppose that the planning authority decides that only a certain number of persons are to be trained in a certain type of skill. This means that if an applicant is not fortunate enough to be accepted within the alloted quota, he has no chance of entry to that occupation. It may perhaps reasonably be pointed out to him that that area is full in the sense that, on the estimates made of demand at certain levels of pay, it is thought that he will have difficulty in getting a job. But what if he declares himself prepared to take the risk? What if he believes that his failure to persuade the authorities concerned is a mistake on their part and he is thus still anxious to get an opportunity of trying? Of course in a free system, where institutions of higher education are free to prescribe what numbers they regard themselves able to accommodate, he may still be unlucky enough to fail to persuade any of them to take him. But it is one thing for free institutions, not acting in concert, to present limits to their own operations. It is quite another thing for the scope they offer to be imposed by a single authority operating from the centre.

But beyond this the general conception of educational planning carries with it, in a broad way, the conception of the direction of labour. The fortunate members of the community quota, once they emerge from training, have to take jobs which are assigned to them.

Doubtless there are some possibilities of evasion – the system is not likely to be 100 per cent efficient. But, as we know from Russian experience, any internal change of interlocal residence is strictly policed. The idea of spontaneous choice and movement is quite foreign to the fundamental principle underlying this practice.

In the final analysis, therefore, it must be clear that the requirement of educational planning and direction of labour is only compatible with that of a totally planned society – a society in which the allocation of resources, the quantities to be produced and the provision to be made for the future are prescribed from a planning organisation at the centre. I would not say that this conception is completely realised in the existing Communist societies; we hear a great deal of the breakdown of plans and the frustration of expectations. And I have no doubt that, in the higher reaches, the allocation of duties and responsibility does not altogether conform to the strict and impersonal principles of impersonal central planning. It is difficult to believe that consideration of party performance and personal affiliation do not play their part here, as in most other forms of human society. The difference in this respect between free societies and Communism is not, that such influences are not present in both, but that, in the one, dispersed initiatives have some opportunity of circumnavigating undesirable obstacles while, in the other, because of the nature of totally centralised control, it is less likely.

Your etc.

5 Grants and Loans

My dear X,

In commenting on my letter on numbers and selection you quite rightly raise the question of the costs involved. To what extent does the provision of places in institutions of higher education entail public expenditure? To what extent should the privileges involved be financed by the beneficiaries? Such problems, even if considered on the plane of the utmost generality – which is all that can be attempted in this correspondence – raise issues of great complexity which certainly deserve a letter to themselves.

I do not think we should be diverted by the problems of education at earlier stages. I presume that most people nowadays would agree that it is right that parents should be obliged to ensure that their children receive education of a kind which meets certain minimum requirements and that it is right too, that where the means of doing so do not exist, then in some way or other they should be provided. Doubtless the way in which provision should be made is still a highly controversial question. On the whole in this country provision has been made *in kind* by the system of state schools: and perhaps yet awhile only a minority – including the present writer – would find more congenial the suggestion of John Stuart Mill that 'if the government would make up its mind to *require* for every child a good education, it might save itself the trouble of *providing* one' by leaving 'to parents to obtain the education where and how they pleased and content itself with helping to pay the school fees of the poorer classes of the community and defraying the entire school expenses of those who have no one else to pay for them'.[1] These are matters which can – and should – still be debated by reasonable people.[2] But opinion is united on the duty of the state, directly or indirectly, to secure primary and secondary education for all the relevant age groups of its citizens.

1. *On Liberty* (Partier, 1859) pp. 190–1.
2. I have dealt with these matters at greater length in my *Political Economy Past & Present* (Macmillan, 1976) pp. 120–3.

But beyond that the problem is different. In this country, at any rate, not all the relevant age groups proceed to higher education: and the universities and the other institutions concerned each have their admission requirements. And this involves costs – the value of services and resources which might otherwise be used elsewhere – for the institution, costs for the creation and maintenance of buildings and equipment plus the more variable element of administration and teaching; and, for the students, the cost of maintenance which, from the social point of view, is, in some sense, not necessarily exactly commensurate with the value of what they could produce if otherwise employed. If one believes that, speaking broadly, society gains from the further education of such members of the relevant age groups, such costs may be regarded as investment in the improvement of human capital for services in the future. Not all this investment may be fruitful, either financially or in terms of wide social benefits. But the fact remains that it involves costs and that these costs are incurred in respect of a limited proportion of the community. How should such expenditure be covered? That is the heart of the problem.

So far as institutions of higher education are devoted to the advancement of knowledge in one shape or another, part of the problem can be conceived to be solved by direct subsidy. To what extent this should be a consumer-producer relationship, to what extent it should be regarded as ministering to less tangible public objectives is clearly a matter about which there can be endless argument. An enquiry concerning the pollution of rivers or the atmosphere can be conceived as appropriately dealt with as falling within the former category. Research into molecular biology, even though it might produce by accident a cure for cancer, or the maintenance of chairs and equipment for archeological research, although in my judgement thoroughly desirable, cannot be so treated. Sensible controversy in this latter connection must clearly relate to matters of degree; and it is a matter for detailed discussion whether, in particular cases, it is underdone – or overdone.

The main problem, however, relates not to scientific research or the advancement of other branches of learning, but rather to the costs of training in the wide sense and the maintenance of those who are being trained.

Here, in the United Kingdom, the prevalent practice is subsidy. In a broad way a substantial part of the expenditure of institutions is borne by grants by various organs of the State – the University

Grants Committee, the Department of Education and Science and, to some extent, Local Government, usually however, itself in receipt of subsidies from the centre. In addition to this and subject to various somewhat complicated means tests, the fees which augment the revenue of the institutions and grants which sustain the students concerned are provided from public finance. I need hardly say that in various ways, both capital accounts and revenues are supplemented by gifts from foundations and individuals and also by the monies provided by the students or the parents who do not survive the means tests. But in the broad perspective these, although by no means negligible, are a minor element in the system. In the United Kingdom at any rate, it is the tax-paying public which, in one way or another, meets the larger part of the costs of training.

Now in so far as all this is to be regarded as capital investment for the future in the very wide sense in which the education of those satisfying suitable admission tests may be so conceived, this mode of provision must be regarded as having substantially beneficial aspects. It certainly makes access to higher education possible for many having the necessary qualifications who, if there were no such sources of finance, would not have such access. It thus satisfies the truly liberal requirement of equality of opportunity at this stage of a young person's career. It deprives the talented offspring of poorer parents of the legitimate complaint that, if they had had support from higher parental income, their chances of success in life would have been greater. In economic terms, it extends the area of access to this part of the investment market.

Unfortunately this benefit has a quite important obverse disadvantage. We may disregard the possibility that it can be financed by printing money: that can happen for a short period but not for long. The investment therefore must be financed, at any rate in periods of reasonably high employment, by other members of the community, i.e. by non-inflationary borrowing or by taxation. That is to say that it can very truthfully be represented as a subsidy paid, to some extent at least, to the relatively clever, or potentially clever, from the relatively not so clever. I do not think that so far it has been widely conceived in these terms – the post-Second World War mythology of the bottomless public purse dies hard. But the fundamental analysis is inescapable; and, as realisation spreads of the increasing burden of public finance, more and more members of the community who do not enjoy such privileges are likely to become aware of it, and to complain.

Confronted with this problem at first sight, the obvious remedy would seem to be the institution of a loan system. If the fundamental inequality of opportunity which the subsidisation of fees and maintenance is designed to remedy, is the unwillingness of the capital market to finance this form of investment, why should not government be willing, directly or indirectly, to make the necessary capital available in this shape? There is a certain crude logic in the suggestion, and, as is well known, to some extent such a system has been adopted in some connections and in some areas. There is also some force in the contention that incurring a loan rather than receiving a subsidy has a beneficial effect on motivation. The student who has incurred liability for a loan, may be argued to have a greater incentive to get value for money than one who receives a free gift.

Unfortunately a simple loan system of this sort is subject to very considerable disadvantages, both administrative and moral. A loan system administered in isolation from the general apparatus of public finance is administratively cumbersome and difficult to run. All existing loan systems known to me present obvious difficulties of collection. Even more important are the moral disadvantages. Not all investment in higher education yields a financial return. Under a simple loan scheme some borrowers may overestimate their eventual earning capacity. Some may choose occupations which have a low pecuniary return. In such cases the repayment of the loan may prove impossible or be attended with exceptional difficulties. The evidence of such arrangements is peculiarly unfair where young women are concerned. It is highly desirable that talented girls should have access to higher education: only educational dinosaurs contend the contrary. But what if, at the end of the course, the girl decides that her vocation is to become a wife and a mother. It is really not an undesirable thing that the mothers of the future who are capable of benefiting from higher education should have the opportunity. But a simple loan scheme constitutes so to speak *a negative dowry*. It is not difficult to conceive of young men of prudence making surreptitious enquiries concerning the indebtedness of possible partners. I cannot believe that that would be a satisfactory state of affairs.

Very fortunately there is a solution to such problems. Professor Prest, an international authority on public finance, supports the general argument which is advanced in favour of loans rather than subsidies. But, recognising the disadvantages which I have just enumerated, he suggests that the problem can be solved by the provision *that repayment shall only be required, if subsequent earnings pass beyond a figure which makes reasonable interest and amortisation possible.* Until then the loan carries with it no liability.

The beauty of this proposal is that it removes both the administrative and moral disadvantages to which simple loan systems are exposed. The administration needs no separate apparatus: it can be part of the normal business of the Inland Revenue authorities; when the earnings of those who have incurred loans exceed the presented figure, collection of the interest and amortisation automatically begins. No special means test, no special machinery for collection is involved. And the moral problem simply disappears. If a talented young man who has incurred a loan decides to go into the Church, and his income in that vocation does not reach the prescribed figure, his liability does not arise. As for the negative dowry for his sister, it does not exist. Only if she decides to engage in pecuniary employment are her earnings taken into account, and then only if they exceed the figure presented for men and women indiscriminately.

The Prest scheme therefore gives us the best of both worlds. By providing the necessary finance by loans rather than subsidies it emphasises the cost of training. At the same time it removes the disincentive to borrow which may arise from fear of eventual inability to repay. For only if future income is such as to make repayment possible, does the liability exist.

How far is it possible to hope that such a scheme should actually come into existence in this country? Clearly its introduction all along the line would have much opposition to overcome. It must be remembered that the policy of wider subsidy preceded the Report on Higher Education. It was the recommendation of Sir Colin Anderson's committee. The Report on Higher Education simply set out, in a somewhat academic way, the arguments for and against subsidies or loans without committing itself to a conclusion. It is a matter of regret to me, personally, that I did not at the time sufficiently appreciate the advantages of the Prest scheme, in spite of the fact that it had been already promulgated. My own inclination tended definitely against the policy of subsidy on the grounds I have already indicated. I was prepared to tolerate it for the time being as encouraging sections of the population which might have been deterred by loans, to contemplate higher education. But I felt that eventually considerations of equity in finance would cause a shift in public opinion. I think some shift has occured: mention of loans no longer encounters the almost universal resistance that was the case in the past. But the Prest modification has not received sufficient publicity; and the grounds on which it removes perfectly legitimate objections to the loan policy, while logically highly cogent, are not such as to be easily grasped in the give and take of discussions which normally take place on this plane.

Moreover, so far as first degrees are concerned, there are further complications to be faced. In so far as forms of education beyond the school-leaving age, other than at universities, are financed from the public purse – which practice is on the increase – a wider selection of the relevant age groups is involved; and the otherwise conclusive objection to subsidy from those who do not qualify for admission to universities to those who do, has less force. I personally would still prefer the extension of the Prest plan to these other areas on the ground that it makes explicit the element of cost. But the argument for the contrary view is not to be dismissed as negligible.

Such complications in the argument of the general case do not, however, apply once the graduate school level is reached. Here is a sphere, even though its extension in certain directions is desirable which must, in the nature of things, be restricted to a comparatively small proportion of the age groups concerned. At the same time it is a sphere where the investment involved, although not inevitably successful from the pecuniary point of view, must in many cases offer the prospect of higher earnings than would otherwise be the case. Such investment therefore, if not eventually repayable, must be regarded as a subsidy from the rest of the community. In periods of financial stringency, it is indeed likely to be curtailed beyond the point at which, taking into account the general interest, it is desirable that it should be so limited.

This indeed is one of the acute problems of our higher education system at the present time. The raising of fees of graduate education, although defensible on many grounds, must certainly reduce the number of applicants to graduate schools who are capable of self-financing. The case for access to the capital expenditure involved is therefore very strong – in all sorts of directions we need more highly trained talent. But, unless this is underwritten by government, the finance will not be forthcoming; and unless the advances take the form of conditionally repayable loans, they are likely to be opposed by large sections of public opinion, some for philistine reasons, some on much more cogent grounds. The finance of graduate education therefore is not only a case where the Prest plan is unequivocally appropriate, it is also a case where it is urgently necessary in the general interest.

Yours etc.

6 Expansion, Motivation and Teaching

My dear X,

In your last letter you return to the question of expansion. You accept, you say, the argument for not raising entrance standards. You do not disagree with my indictment of the undesirability of high specialisation at an early age and you tolerate, at least, my somewhat complicated assessment of the relative merits of subsidies and loans as methods of meeting the costs of expansion. But you now point out that, whatever I have said regarding the arguments for expansion and the methods it should involve, I have not yet revealed my view of the *results* of expansion. Accepting the case against *raising* the difficulties of admission you ask whether the expansion has not in fact *lowered* the standards actually prevailing. Have not entrance standards actually been lowered? And, even if this has not happened, what are we to say of the frame of mind of the enlarged student population – have standards been maintained in that sense? What have been the effects of increases in the size of departments and universities as a whole? And what about the increase of student militancy in various shapes and forms?

These are questions more delicate than those we have discussed up to now and it may easily take several letters to answer them. But they are certainly very pertinent. The case for expansion may have been very cogent. But the proof of the pudding is in the eating; and our correspondence would be totally unbalanced if we did not look at the results. In this letter I will discuss entrance standards, motivation and teaching.

As regards entrance standards I think you may put your mind at rest. As you know, I detest premature specialisation at school and I have no doubt that our general cultural standards have been seriously imperilled by the insistence of many university departments South of the Border upon grades in prescribed A levels as an essential qualification for admission to their courses. But this does not mean a relaxation of academic requirements in such tests. Indeed I have the impression – and it is only an impression – that in various ways nowadays, it is harder, rather than easier, to gain entrance to universities. Certainly, in my now limited experience as a teacher, in the years since 1963 I have noticed no falling off of the intellectual ability of the first degree students with whom I have had contact. The belief, so strongly presented by Sir Claus Moser and Mr Richard Layard, that there was an increasing potential of young persons with the capacity to satisfy entrance requirements of undiminished severity has been justified so far as my observation goes.

This is not to say, however, that the situation is entirely satisfactory. At most times and in most universities, I suppose, there must have been students who, for one reason or another, felt that they had mistaken their vocation, students who, even after the natural initial difficulties of accommodating themselves to new companions, new expectations regarding work, and a new intellectual and social atmosphere, remained bewildered and ill at ease. To some extent this is inevitable. Let the framers of examination questions be never so ingenious, let the interviewers be never so acute, the stop-watch psychological merchants be never so assiduous and the school reports be never so perceptive and candid, the assessment of future performance is bound to be wrong sometimes. The teacher who claims he has never made a mistake in this respect writes himself down in my eyes as a fool or a fraud. So some people are admitted who probably should be better advised to stay away, just as some people are rejected who may have had adequate and indeed splendid potential. This is a fact of life, likely to persist in the best organised system.

Nevertheless I cannot resist the feeling that with the expansion, there are proportionately more of such misfits than formerly. Again I should warn you that this is an impressionistic judgement; it does not claim to be vindicated by quantitative surveys, which incidentally, in my opinion, would present quite peculiar difficulties in this connection. All the same, it is certainly my belief, based not merely on personal contacts but on conversations with experienced teachers, that increasing numbers have been accompanied by proportionately more bewilderment, lack of sense of purpose and positive discontent than formerly. It would be hazardous to put a percentage figure on it. As I shall be arguing, the causes are multiple and doubtless vary in different institutions. But that the proportionate increase is considerable seems to me to be clear; and, although I would contest the view that it is the main cause of increased student militancy, I think it is arguable that it is one of the elements in which such manifestations develop.

Why is this? I can think of a variety of influences. The very fact of expansion tended to make it fashionable. The availability of subsidy must have opened the eyes of many parents who otherwise would not have contemplated a period of university education for their off-spring – not a bad influence in general, even if it led to some mistakes. Emulation: the fact that other school-fellows were going up may have prompted applications on the part of some who were in fact temperamentally unsuited to follow their example. I am also tempted to believe that the universities themselves, while guiltless of lowering admission standards, may have tended to over-state the value of this kind of training. 'Dad said I should never get an income of over £1500 a year unless I had a university degree' said one of the unfortunate disillusioned to one of my colleagues, at a time when £1500 a year still meant something. I certainly know various people who have done very well for themselves and for others, who have nevertheless a sense of inferiority for not having been at a university – a point of view which, on my scale of values, is quite unwarranted – and their attitude may have inspired advice which was unsuitable for those to whom it was given. The criteria for the availability of places recommended by the Committee on Higher Education included not only the *ability* but also the *willingness* to take advantage of the opportunity; and in the event the willingness has sometimes proved illusory.

Now I have no doubt that some of this sense of frustration and bewilderment can be remedied by better organisation of supervision and teaching. Supervision at the early stage of transition from school to university is very important although very frequently neglected; and there is much need for closer attention to the ordering of lectures and to the technique of delivering them. The belief that academic standing derived from intellectual excellence confers immunity from the requirement of a minimum efficiency in communication, which seems to prevail among too many university teachers, is certainly responsible for some removable perplexity and discontent among students. It is also responsible for the contention, quite widely held in some quarters, that, given the existence of good text-books, there is no need for oral instruction, which for anyone who has had the good fortune to hear efficient lecturing is palpable nonsense. I am not in favour of long pretentious courses of education for university educators. But I do believe that the virtually total neglect of attention to the business of arrangement and delivery which undoubtedly exists among many university teachers – in Britain as distinct from France – has a lot to answer for. A good lecture can be an inspiration; a bad lecture an insufferable bore.

I am also inclined to think that more consideration should be given to the timing and nature of examinations. I can well understand the case for leaving potential firsts, i.e. those who are likely to achieve actual firsts or good upper seconds, to get on with the job of soaking themselves in their subjects, untroubled by the shadow of near examinations. I remember, as a student, myself heading a deputation to this effect to the authorities at the London School of Economics. But in first degrees, I would now argue that the appropriate pedagogic target for teaching and arrangement of work is not the potential first but rather the average second, who after all has to do much of the main work of the university-trained world; and for these there is much to be said for the view that frequent examinations are a powerful incentive not to waste time at the beginning, leaving too much to be done in a panic towards the end. On balance, therefore, I do believe that, with an enlarged university population, there is much to be gained by adoption of something like the American credit system whereby, if the student wishes to do well, he is kept up to the mark from the beginning. More protracted lingering over matters of arresting interest is much more suited for the gifted minority who survive to the graduate school stage.

But when all is said and done to improve the teaching and guidance in universities, I cannot resist the impression that there will still be left among the proportionately enlarged student numbers – which I welcome – a not insubstantial residue of young people who, whatever their talents in other respects, had better have chosen otherwise. And, in such cases, I feel that the fundamental trouble is the necessity of premature choice and the absence of introspective knowledge of their own prospective potentialities and inclinations. The immediate transition from school to university obliges them to make a decision before they know what they really want.

In support of this diagnosis I would appeal to the experience of two wars and their aftermath. Every close observer of the university scene would testify that if a young person, man or woman, having been caught up in National Service for a period, then decided to embark on university training he, or she, had a very fair notion of what that involved and what he or she desired to get out of it. *Au contraire* where that was not so, there was much more uncertainty. I suspect that, with the enlarged opportunities, this was even more so after the Second World War than after the First. Indeed for those of us who were teaching at that time, the cessation of National Service created, so to speak, *a watershed* in the attitude of many students. While National Service prevailed, an application for admission usually meant a deliberate choice and purpose. When it ceased, there was much less deliberation and much more ambiguity of expectations.

This is not a plea for the revival of National Service, though I confess that, considering the present perilous state of international relations, I should not regard it as undesirable that we were that much better able to defend ourselves, perhaps by training on Swiss lines. But it is a plea for consideration to be given to the desirability of some interval between school leaving and entering a university, or indeed any full-time course at an institute of higher education. Is there not something to be said for a period in which, before commitment to such a rarefied world, the young person may have the opportunity of mixing with others who are not so committed, and of discovering whether he or she really wishes the ardours and endurances that that involves. The idea is not novel. Something of the sort was recommended as long ago as Plato. It is actually put into practice, perhaps in an extreme manner and for somewhat fanciful idealogical reasons, in the Soviet Union at the present day; and in the Western world, when this kind of delay has been imposed by military necessity, it has not proved disastrous.

Now of course, there are subjects where continuity of study is desirable – music or pure mathematics, for example. I would not like to be thought to be advocating an interval of knocking about in either National Service or miscellaneous activities in industry, commerce or agriculture for, say, Mozart or Einstein. But, in between such limiting cases, in the broad band of scientific or humanistic subjects, what harm can there be in coming to them later after some experience of non-academic life and some opportunity of discovering what one really wants? I simply do not believe that, save in exceptional subjects where exceptional qualifications could be ascertained by appropriate tests, any harm would be done by a policy of no grants – or loans – before the age of 20; and I suspect that, in that way, a substantial proportion of misfits would be avoided, with all the waste and unhappiness that it implies.

Apart from superior knowledge of their own inclinations and the demands made upon them there would be a further advantage in entry at a somewhat later stage: the students would have a stronger sense of independent initiative and a stronger sense of compulsion to get on with work for themselves.

At once I hasten to say that, speaking generally, I do think that students, of whatever age, do not receive enough supervision of the right kind nowadays – if you tempted me, I could say a good deal of the deficiencies on the teaching side in many institutions; and perhaps there may be an opportunity later on. But whatever one can say of the present generation of students – and in many ways I think them certainly as intelligent and perceptive as their predecessors – I do not think it can be said that all of them have the same disposition to do things for themselves. The constant demand for '*the* tutorial system' is evidence of that; and by '*the* tutorial system' is meant the one-to-one relationship which used to be prevalent at Oxford and Cambridge. Now the plain fact is that the thorough going one-to-one relationship, with each student entitled to a whole hour's undivided attention once or twice a week from his tutors, although at some stages desirable in the graduate school, is simply not generally practicable at the first degree stage with an enlarged university population; and while there is often still great need to improve some sort of personal supervision of such students, especially at the beginning stages, there is, I would say, an equal need for students to realise that it is the essence of university study that the tutors are not there to deal with *all* personal problems and that some spontaneity in the planning of programmes and the sense of obligation to work is necessary and incumbent. I do not think that any sympathetic teacher who has watched the activities of beginners at the respective ages of 17 to 19 and 19 to 21 or 22 can doubt that, in this respect, the advantage lies usually with the latter group. I certainly remember that when, as an ex-soldier after the First World War, I returned to university studies at LSE, I only saw a tutor once in the first year; and, as my recollection goes, our conversation was restricted to an inquiry about whether I was interested in sport and an invitation to tea – which was never followed up. I felt no special deprivation at this, and indeed, some sense of relief; whereas when, at a preternaturally early age, I attended another college for a term or two before joining the army, I felt very acutely the need of more supervision than I received.

Thus, if my suggestion of a period in the world at large before proceeding to full-time higher education were adopted – which, having regard to the frame of mind of school-masters, parents and the young people themselves, is highly improbable – it would kill two birds with one stone. It would diminish the number of entrants who, for one reason or another, were temperamentally unsuitable; and, from the word go, it would increase the proportion of students capable, to the extent desirable, of looking after themselves and conscious of the urgent need to make the most of every hour available.

Yours etc.

7 The Size of University Institutions

My dear X,

In commenting on my remarks about motivation and teaching you raise the problem of the appropriate size of university institutions. This is an acute point, if I may say so, since although, given the historical situation in this and many other countries, there is probably little that can be done in the near future in the way of radical change, I do think that there are real connections between size and other factors determining the efficiency of such institutions; and there are quite a number of aspects of this matter which should be in the minds of those who, later on, may be responsible for policy.

Let me begin my thoughts on this subject by disentangling the nature of the problem. University institutions are not all similar in their coverage and objectives. Some may include the whole range of faculties – to use the word in its specifically British setting. Others may be deliberately limited to a more restricted sphere; and, of course, such *horizontal* differences will affect the desirable size of the institutions concerned. Furthermore some institutions may specialise to a much larger extent than others on graduate studies and research. And such *vertical* differences may carry with them different requirements of staff, students and equipment and therefore influence the size that is to be deemed appropriate.

Nevertheless there are problems concerning size *as such*, although, as I shall argue, even here the desirable solutions may be multiple. But it is certainly not unintelligible to inquire whether, given their coverage and objectives, the efficiency of institutions may not vary with their size. That is to say it is a real question whether a university may not be too small or too large.

I do not think that I need to linger over criteria of insufficient size. No matter how limited the range of subjects, there must be a minimum of appropriate material provision, library and laboratory facilities, etc. and a minimum division of labour among the staff if

45

good standards are to be established. I conjecture that, with the growth of knowledge, even with the limited objective of instructions for first degrees, such minima have been substantially raised in the last century; and, in this way, even with very low staff/student ratios, an institution might gain positively from being larger.

There is also the consideration of minimum mixture. A great deal of nonsense is talked about the desirability of multiplicity of faculties – again using the word in the British sense – in order to promote 'cross-fertilisation', an exchange of views between those pursuing different subjects. I am quite sure from experience that it is not necessary to have all conceivable faculties within one institution claiming university status, for opportunities to exist for sufficient cross-fertilisation. It is preposterous to argue that in order to create an adequate university atmosphere, it is necessary to have law, medicine, engineering, natural science, economics, etc. all under one roof; and, of course, where they are, extensive cross-fertilisation is not necessarily as frequent as is sometimes claimed. But there is still something in the contention that some diversity is desirable, if only to guard against excessive specialisation at the first degree stage. I am sure that restriction to single or a very narrow range of subjects, while often appropriate to graduate institutions, is too narrow a basis for first degree training. This is another reason why universities can be conceived to be too small.

In my judgement however, this is not a very great danger – except perhaps when new universities are being started. Academics – or at least a considerable number of them – are not unambitious. For those who have such a disposition, the desire to expand is often a very strong motive indeed; and in a considerable number of cases it succeeds. Much more important therefore than the danger that universities may be too small is the danger that they may be too large. They may be too large as regards staff, as regards students and as regards administration.

Take first the problem of staffing. This is a matter of arithmetic. An effective staff must know each other and be subject to some degree of cooperative organisation. If a department comprises, say, 20 members with different grading and different potentialities and a turnover of, perhaps, 2 per session, it is possible – and, of course, highly desirable – that whoever is chairman of the department may get to know intimately the hopes and fears and the academic and administrative potential of its various members. Moreover with a small turnover, he will be able speedily to induct the newcomers about whom presumably he will already have made himself reasonably well informed, into the atmosphere of the department. If, however, the department comprises, let us say, 60 members with an annual turnover of, say at least 10 – which will sometimes be the case in such circumstances – such intimate knowledge and such special attention is quite out of the question. The various members themselves hardly know intimately more than a fraction of their colleagues. As for the chairman, it is physically quite impossible for him to be personally aware of the academic, let alone the personal, potential of those in respect of whom he frequently has to make quite important decisions.

The student problem is even more evident. In comparatively small institutions or departments even at the beginning, the student can be made to feel that he somehow 'belongs'. Once numbers have passed a certain level, however, there is a danger that he may feel himself an atom in a bewildering world of otherwise discrete atoms; and although he may eventually find some place in accidental groupings, the atmosphere is not the same. I know that when I have visited some of the more gigantic American universities, justly renowned for their achievements in graduate training and research with vast numbers of Nobel prize winners on the campus, I have felt that, if I were to be the parent of some young person living in the neighbourhood, I would much prefer to send him to a small local liberal arts college for the first degree, leaving the more prestigious contacts for later on. He would not necessarily have such distinguished senior lecturers. But the general atmosphere would be more congenial to balanced development.

Finally administration. Doubtless it is not necessary that all members of the academic staff should be concerned with academic organisation. But a certain degree of involvement, especially on the part of persons with senior responsibility, is desirable if matters are not to be left to a dictatorial administration. If the institution passes a certain size, the burden of work becomes excessive, even for those who tend to enjoy this sort of thing and are good at it. As for the evolution of policy, if it is to be carried on with some show of general consent, the meetings first become too large for reasonable discussion; and eventually a certain proportion of the more sensible members of the eligible members of staff tend to stay away, preferring to get on with what they regard as more important work. This is a very real danger.

Now doubtless these difficulties can be reduced by well-considered organisation. The troubles of heads of departments can be mitigated by some devolution of responsibility for allocation of work and personal contacts. The bewilderment and perplexities of students can be dealt with by suitable, and not necessarily wasteful, tutorial systems, small classes and so on. The administrative burden can be eased by the academics reposing more trust in professional administrators and some prudent birth-control in regard to the multiplication of committees. I suspect that a substantial proportion of university institutions in this country, whatever their size, could increase their efficiency by improvements in these directions. Certainly the administrative efficiency of academic institutions is far less than in reputable private enterprise and even in government offices.

Nevertheless, in greater or less degree, once a certain size, appropriate to the objective of the university concerned, has been passed, whatever has been done to stiffen up existing practices in regard to staff, students and administration, diminishing returns begin to operate. The atmosphere becomes more and more impersonal. The sense of corporate loyalty among all but the most dedicated members of the staff tends to wane and attention is concentrated more and more on individual research. The students never acquire that feeling of corporate 'belonging' which, where it prevails, is such an addition to the amenities of existence; and administration tends to become a job unconnected with the real *raison d'être* of such a society. Thus there arises a weariness of the flesh due to the lack of any spontaneous sense of affiliation among staff and students. It is difficult to put a figure on the point at which this begins to become obvious. But in a *unitary* university with a multiplicity of faculties, I would begin to see the red light when numbers were much above 5000.

I say *unitary* university: for I certainly believe that there is plenty of scope for greater size, at any rate for student-staff problems, in a *collegiate* system – where the university is composed of a series of quasi-independent colleges to which each individual student and teacher is automatically assigned. I say quasi-independent to distinguish the system I have in mind from the existing systems of Oxford and Cambridge where each college is an independent legal entity – an arrangement which certainly works well enough in those ancient universities as it has been modified by history but which, with the present system of university finances, it is impossible to conceive of being reproduced, at any rate here in the United

Kingdom in the twentieth century. But the analogy has its positive as well as negative lessons. The collegiate system at Oxford and Cambridge is undoubtedly infinitely superior to the unitary system on the side of human relationships; and, administratively, I do not think it has suffered too much from the multiplication of colleges. I find it no accident that, although the physical results of student militancy have been probably at least as great at the ancient universities as elsewhere – at Cambridge they burnt a hotel, at Oxford they did extensive damage to the Examination Schools – yet at neither place did it seem to threaten the continuity or general repute of the system. Indeed, on the whole it didn't get into the papers as much as considerably less damage perpetrated elsewhere. The college system goes on in circumstances where a unitary institution of more than a certain size can be paralysed. Personally, having had the privilege of being partly responsible for the planning of the University of York, I should not be alarmed if it extended to more than its existing number of colleges; whereas, if it were unitary, I should begin to think that it was time to call a halt.

Needless to say the collegiate system has its difficulties. It clearly should involve an inter-collegiate superstructure in the different faculties or sub-faculties to arrange for an orderly lecture list – which certainly was not always the case in Economics at Oxford in my time in the 1920s. Where graduate work involves apparatus of one kind or another, it also involves some super-collegiate organisation, not, I think, necessarily very difficult to improvise. And where the colleges are not legal entities, as with new universities in the modern age, it is difficult to conceive otherwise, the university must exercise financial controls in its allocations. I would not argue that a quasi-collegiate system is free from administrative complications. But I would certainly argue that these are far outweighed by the advantages of smaller units and the immense human gain of closer relations between staff and students within these units.

A collegiate system must be distinguished from federal systems as university terminology goes. Federal systems prevail where the units, which may well be as large as typical universities, are linked together by a common government. Here I suspect that the balance of advantage goes the other way. In efficient administration, propinquity is overwhelmingly important. A satisfactory university spirit cannot be evoked when the administrators and senior teachers involved have to travel miles and miles to take part in common committees; still less when they do not meet but are bound by detailed regulations concocted in some centre which they never or seldom enter. To speak of a university in such circumstances seems to me to convey a very misleading impression.

You may ask, in the light of these strictures, what then of the University of London? Here is a cluster of colleges and institutions, several of which are in numbers equivalent to provincial universities, situated indeed in the London or Greater London area and in different degrees subject to a central administrative body at Bloomsbury. Well, in the days before the mid-1960s, this degree of tutelage was becoming more and more irksome to some of the larger colleges concerned. In the report of the Committee on Higher Education some allusion was made to these problems; and I confess that when I wrote the sentences involved – which it has been revealed, not by me, that I did – I feared that some break-up was inevitable although, for reasons that I will shortly disclose, I personally would have regretted it. In fact that has not happened. By an effort which at the time I should not have thought to be probable, a committee under the inspiration of Sir Douglas Logan, the then Principal, and Professor Saunders of Imperial College, brought about changes which in effect conferred what might be called Dominion Status on the larger institutions; and the movement towards separatism which was very strong, has died down. There may be some controls remaining which are thought to be irksome. But in effect the major restraints have been removed; and, in many important respects, the larger institutions can function as if they were independent universities.

What then is the continuing justification for the continuance of the central organisation? In my judgement it lies mainly in the existence of the congeries of specialised institutions which have grown up under the direct aegis of the university – the Institute of Historical Studies, the Institute of Advanced Legal Studies, the Courtauld Institute and so on. These institutes are world famous for their scholarship and teaching; and they continually attract a very high grade clientele from all over the civilised world. Yet it is clear that, even the largest of the large colleges, University College itself, could not possibly maintain even one or two of them independently: and their disintegration or their financial starvation would be a major academic disaster. Needless to say one can think of other ways of looking after them. But it would take many years to acquire the drive; and in my view it would be a great folly to disturb existing arrangements. If the University of London had done nothing else good – and of course at earlier times its external examination system was an immense contribution to higher education, not only in this country but in the greater part of the English-speaking world at large – it would deserve high credit for the way in which it has nurtured these institutions.

Yours etc.

8 Student Militancy and Unrest

My dear X,

You keep plugging away at the deterioration of the quality of student life which you seem to believe has accompanied expansion; and, in your last letter, you refer to the outbursts of student militancy which have attracted so much public attention in the last ten years or so. This is a challenge which must be met; and it so happens that it concerns matters of which I have had intimate personal experience in more than one connection. Let me say at once that I share your concern at what has happened. But I doubt whether you have the right perspective; and this will take some space to elaborate. I can only ask you, in the words of Brutus in *Julius Caesar*, to 'Be patient to the last'.

Let me say at once that I am not unaware of the truly shocking nature which student militancy has assumed in the last twelve years in this country. It is not so novel elsewhere and in the past there were isolated instances here. But the width and nature of the disturbances here of the late 1960s and early 1970s had no precedent in our history. Complete interruption of orderly teaching and administration, occupation of college buildings often attended with destruction of property, walls defaced by obscene inscriptions and denunciations, meetings, intended for reasonable discussion, rendered chaotic by shouts and stamping, women administrators who had endeavoured to penetrate to their offices to get on with the work of their institution, knocked down and physically injured, a private house broken into and the contents rifled in search of official documents, vice-chancellors locked into their rooms, their private papers stolen and circulated to all and sundry – these are episodes to deal with which prominent public figures, without troubling themselves to make the slightest investigation of the facts, urged conciliation and even, from time to time, laid the blame on the victims. From this condemnation I think it only just to exempt the then Secretary of State for Education and Science (at that time Mr Short, now Lord Glenamara), who, in one instance went out of his way to describe the rebels as 'thugs' and assured those concerned with the re-establishment of order of any help within his power – a striking contrast with the Laodicean attitude of some who might have been expected to show concern. I knew intimately one head of a university who died of a heart attack directly traceable to the *sequelae* of such events. I know of another who died prematurely, probably because of the strains arising from such anxieties. No one who lived through this period associated with the universities concerned, with any regard for their reputation and order, can look back to such manifestations without a sense of pollution.

But having said this, let me also make clear by way of preliminary comment, that this is *not* – I repeat *not* – the indictment of a generation. I firmly believe that by far the greater majority of university students of today are as decent, as friendly and as intelligent as their predecessors and many, if not all, make at least as good use of their time. It is absolutely unjust that they should be stigmatised with the stain of these disturbing occurrences. On one occasion when my own lectures were interrupted by a disorderly gang demanding 'to make a statement', I held a vote asking whether it was desired that I should continue the lecture on Ricardo's Theory of Profit or whether the interruption should be allowed. Every hand in the room was raised for continuation; there was no support whatever for the intruders. I think there are problems about the attitude of the generality of students which I will touch upon shortly. But any belief that the downright evils of militancy are due to the majority can only be held by those who are ignorant of the facts – a surprising proportion of the electorate. The press and the media have a very poor record in this respect, giving great prominence to small incidents and rebellious personalities while, for the most part, revealing little of the true perspective of what was going on. A silly boy has only to burn an examination paper on the steps of some institution and all the television cameras and the more imbecile reporters – duly notified of course by the persons concerned – are on the spot while the most shocking outrages to persons and property go unnoticed or, alternatively, are attributed to widespread and legitimate grievances which a more sympathetic understanding on the part of 'the authorities' might have eliminated.

To establish some sense of proportion in these matters, it is necessary to conceive of the student body as falling into at least three divisions – needless to say, changing in numbers and the persons concerned from year to year, but, roughly speaking, identifiable in their respective attitudes.

First come the greater proportion who are more or less indifferent, save in so far as they are personally inconvenienced by overt manifestations of militancy, hardly ever take any part in student politics – and are indeed thoroughly bored by them. If any of this group, out of curiosity, look in at union meetings, seldom attended by more than a quarter of the student body, after enduring say an hour of more or less pointless talk about constitutional minutiae or points of order, they are apt to steal away and get on with their work in lecture-rooms or in libraries. It is important to recognise that such attitudes are typical of a large majority, and also to realise that this attitude is a comparatively recent development. Indeed I would be disposed to argue that the indifference of the majority to what goes on in such connections is one of the genuinely *new* problems of the enlarged universities. Perhaps it derives from the consequences of increased size to which I drew your attention in my last letter. At any rate I am pretty sure that, in the interwar period, the average student would not have been so passive as his successors, if confronted with disturbances which might affect the reputation of *his* institution and consequently his *own* prospects. Indeed, if my recollection of those days does not betray me, the pendulum was often definitely on the opposite side; there was a good deal of interference with what I should have regarded as harmless eccentricities on the part of various minorities and perhaps some distasteful persecution.

Secondly we must take note of a not inconsiderable band of volatile high-spirited youth, unreflecting if you like, but generous and apt to go off at half-cock at any suggestion of abuse of authority. I can best illustrate this attitude by an incident in which I was personally involved.

It was at the time of the first so-called 'troubles' at LSE which concerned the election to the Directorship of the late Sir Walter Adams of whom it was alleged that, in his administration of the University College at Salisbury, Rhodesia, he had shown himself to be a 'racist'. Now in fact there was not a scintilla of truth in this accusation whose basis, if it had any but purely malicious intention, was that, confronted by insults and persecution by the rebel government of that country, he had refused to shut down the college and thus deprive the unfortunate blacks of the one opportunity of getting a first-class university education in that part of the world. I fancy that Adams' greatest friends would not have regarded him as the world's best administrator. But of racism there was not the faintest taint in his make-up. On the contrary, in his young days when university posts were hard to come by, he had resigned his lectureship at University College, London, in order to act as secretary to the committee formed by Beveridge, A. V. Hill and others to assist refugees from central Europe at the time of the Hitler abomination: there must still be very many distinguished scholars of Jewish origin, who owe their second careers and perhaps more than that, their personal safety to Adams' dedicated efforts. This, however, did not inhibit the extremists from organising 'sit-ins' and demonstrations in the course of one of which a uniformed attendant, a devoted servant of the School who had a weak heart, collapsed and died, not indeed of physical assault but of anxiety and excitement – an event certainly not unconnected with the disorder thus provoked.

But more of the extremist mentality later on; my present concern is with decent, misguided people. At the time of these troubles I, being then a part-time lecturer, found myself in a lift with a group – three or four – of students who knew me through attending a course which I was then delivering; and one of them inquired what I thought of what was going on. 'If I may speak candidly', I replied, 'I think it is truly deplorable'. 'Well we don't' was the comment. At which I suggested that we should get out of the lift and talk it out. They agreed amicably enough to do this; and, re-established on *terra firma*, I said 'Well, if you don't think it deplorable to describe as a racist a man who gave up a promising academic career to help victims of totalitarian tyranny I just don't understand your approach'. 'Oh we don't know anything about that' was the response. 'We were only told that some students were being unjustly treated and *we thought it would be dishonourable not to participate in the protest*' (my italics). I think this is utterly typical of by far the greater number of demonstrating students. As is well known to any sympathetic observer, young people are highly sensitive to any suggestion of injustice, however slender the evidence, and highly suspicious of authority: and at the present time, with the quite obvious lowering of the quality and intelligence of public life and the fearful uncertainties of the international position, many of the more highly spirited are at once anxious and apt prey for any suggestion of arbitrary behaviour or neglect on the part of those responsible for orderly administration. I would also add that, for some of them at least, any sort of participation in mass demonstration is a certain release of the soul: an unreflecting feeling of togetherness is an enlivening experience both for those who are naturally gregarious and for some of those who are apt to be lonely.

Let me now come to the third group, the extremists, the very deliberate and dedicated organisers of trouble. It is quite fundamental to understand that these are a very small proportion of the typical total student body. In an institution with which I am well acquainted, I am sure that it would be an exaggeration to put them at a 100 out of a population of over 3000. And even here there is not homogeneity. I would think that quite a number of such a group would eventually grow out of their infatuations and become reasonable members of a free society – whatever political parties they eventually belong to. After all, one must always remember what silly obsessions so many of us ourselves have had when young; and, although I would not make this an excuse for some of the things which such persons have done recently in conjunction with the probable irredeemables, I think it calls for a certain reserve in making sweeping judgements about the future of members of the group as a whole.

But what are the characteristics in action which distinguish members of this group from the excitable, volatile and confused group who are often their followers? This is not an easy question to answer, although if one has lived· through one of these manifestations, the general atmosphere is unmistakable judged by normal human values. Perhaps the first thing that comes to mind is an almost total unwillingness to engage in reasonable argument. However friendly the attempt to discuss the ostensible reason for dispute on its merits, the response is almost invariably the dogmatic reiteration of wooden slogans, at best remotely relevant to the subject under discussion and often not even that. This might charitably be attributed to imperfect understanding; a proportion of such groups, although by no means all, are apt to be neither subtle nor even very bright. But this is only the beginning. A certain amount of misrepresentation of the other side of the case is not infrequent in all sorts of disputes. But complete distortion of fact goes beyond this; and anyone acquainted with the broadsheets allegedly descriptive of the attitude of 'the authorities', secretly printed and distributed to all and sundry by active militants will recognise the moderation of this statement. No member of a staff or governing body who attempts to negotiate can expect to be free from this sort of thing, coupled with innuendo and abuse. Incitement to destruction of property is not infrequent: at a public meeting an extremist in one dispute proposed the burning of a world famous library 'as a gesture'. The theft of private papers often takes place; so does the total suppression by clamour of public meetings to which exception is taken; last but not least threats to individuals – all such expedients are taken as legitimate in the war against '*the* system' – whatever that may mean. It is difficult to find short formulae to describe the various psychological attitudes involved in the initiation of these evils. But that they are ugly and totally incompatible with the desirable ethos of universities is incontestable.

What were the ultimate issues involved in the militancy of the late 1960s? To judge by chance reports in the press, it might appear that they were very miscellaneous – a chance coincidence of disparate grievances, the fault usually of 'the authorities' not to have foreseen or remedied. But so far as the central body of the extremists were concerned, we have a very authoritative account of their ultimate intentions by a certain Dr Paul Hoch, an American, who, although registered at Bedford College, was confessedly one of the main leaders in the troubles of 1968–9 at LSE and in London University generally. In a work written in collaboration with a Mr Victor Schoenbach, a fellow-countryman, entitled *L.S.E.: the Natives are Restless* we find the following *confessio fide*

We should not think of ourselves as militant trade unionists nursing the seeds of revolt in a particular factory but as students *temporarily* at a particular institution and concerned with inspiring people there *and elsewhere* to higher levels of militancy. In this view it is important that our actions be *credible* to the mass of students, but not necessarily that we achieve Union mandates for them, or run candidates in Union elections or infiltrate the NUS (the latest IS+ idea). The only way we are going to break down the fear most people have about revolutionary action is to begin to take such actions ourselves.

Dr Hoch certainly had the courage of his convictions. Later on he was sentenced to nine months' imprisonment and recommended for deportation for unlawful assembly and assault at the Senate House of the University of London.

Student power – that was clearly the objective underlying the acts and stratagems of the inner groups of student militancy in the disturbed days of the late 1960s and early 1970s, and, in so far as such tendencies still lurk beneath the surface in this country, as I think they do, it is the residue of the ideology involved which inspires the more active and dedicated spirits.

But what does it mean? There will be much to be said about various demands for student representation if this correspondence leads to discussions of university government. But the demand for student power as formulated on the part of the extremists of those days, although not altogether unrelated, went much further than that. It meant the assumption of responsibility for the running of all branches of university activity on the part of an alleged democracy. '*Either we take over or they close down*' was the slogan of those days. This meant control of curricula, appointment of teachers, responsibility for internal and external administration. To write this down calmly makes it sound silly. But to anyone who lived through such episodes, there can be no doubt of the intensity of the emotions inspiring it, nor the types of action, including deliberate untruth and the practice of violence which it seemed to justify. Seldom, in our society at least, can there have been instances where the maxim 'the end justifies the means' was more dominant in action. The frame of mind from which all this springs deserves some further examination.

Let me begin with the tactics adopted. The general strategy of student power may well be the underlying motive. But it seldom comes into the open where the immediate grounds of agitation are concerned. Issues such as the price of food in the canteens, the rent of residences, rumours of injustice, such as in the episode related earlier, investments of various kinds deemed likely to be unpopular, political decisions considered to be adverse to higher education – however much members of the staff and administration may have been foremost in opposing them – such like matters are represented as calling for mass demonstrations, sit-ins, occupation of administrative offices and so on.

Moreover quite considerable ingenuity is exhibited in the timing of such agitations. In the Michaelmas term they are comparatively infrequent or seldom reach full force; there has not been time to attempt to indoctrinate the freshers – one-third of the undergraduate body. In the summer term only the most dedicated extremists will be distracted from examinations. Clearly then *a priori* the Lent term should be the most favourable period; and experience shows that it is. It is certainly the time in which what I have called the second band, the volatile and unreflecting, are most vulnerable to be roused to protest against alleged grievances.

At the same time, while, in the day-to-day tactics of conflict, very considerable ingenuity is displayed by some of the characters concerned, not to mention any advisers who may have been behind the battle, it is accompanied, at any rate among the more sincere, by the most astonishing naïveté of conceptions. The following scrap of dialogue, though it never took place in so many words, is not unfair a reconstruction of this attitude of mind.

A defender of the Institution Concerned: Now we have got together for a drink, let's have a grown-up talk about the nature of your objectives. Suppose that we were to give in to your demands, how would you run the place?

A Rebel: We should run it democratically. We *believe* in democracy you know. And that means *all* the people in the place, students, clerks, uniformed attendants, cleaners – and any of you teachers who cared to come and participate on a democratic basis.

The Defender: You do realise don't you, that that would be physically impossible. The largest lecture room here only holds some 800 and there must be more than 4500 bodies about the place.

The Rebel: Well there are overflow rooms which could be wired up – as they have been for one or two public lectures – or we could hire accommodation outside.

The Defender: I doubt if the wiring up works both ways. As for the outside accommodation, have you ever seen a gathering of 4500 people in conclave? You don't get down to administrative detail that way. Tell me, for instance, how would you decide on your agenda? How would you elect your executive committee?

The Rebel: Executive committee? That's just what we want to get away from. Standing committees get entrenched. They lose touch with their constituents. *We should deal with each problem as it came up by ad hoc committees democratically elected.*

I must emphasise that I never participated in such a conversation. But piecing together talks which I have had with many who maintained such contacts, I do not think for a moment that it could not have happened. And I am quite sure that it is the logical implication of a great deal that I myself read or heard said.

So it was such a combination of lack of scruple and simplistic anticipation of future possibilities which was at the heart of student militancy.

How far has all this been suggested or supported from outside? It would be hazardous to profess any certainty in this respect. But there are, however, considerable grounds for some such belief. The choice of common subjects for agitation in different parts of the country although arousing suspicion is not definite proof: the alleged grievances may be spontaneously and simultaneously felt; and there is a tendency for fashions to spread. Much more tangible evidence is provided by the appearance at demonstrations and such like protests of unfamiliar faces, faces which prove to be from other colleges or universities. I would be fairly sure that extremist groups in various parts of the higher education system in London maintain some sort of contact with each other; and, in another area, I myself was present at a disturbing riot where, of some 200 active participants, competent judges regarded at least 50 as coming from outside.

But this does not necessarily indicate a continuing system, and indeed there are some grounds for considerable scepticism in this respect. I have no doubt that members of the Communist party have continuing contacts. But extremists quarrel among themselves. There is obviously not much amity between Trotskyites and Communists; and the International Socialists are sometimes denounced by other groups. It is probable that particular episodes may induce temporary alliances. But this is no proof of the existence of continuing and systematic plans for producing trouble. What is clear, however, is that, in the present climate of political opinion, various extremist groups regard the universities and polytechnics as particularly fruitful ground for propaganda and agitation and act accordingly. It would be difficult to think of any of the more flagrant cases of continuing student disorder where there has not been some indication of this sort.

It would be a great mistake, however, in this general survey, to concentrate solely on the handful of extremists, and their attitudes. Ours is an age of anxiety; the younger you are the more sensitive you are apt to be to this atmosphere. This underlines not only the attitudes of extremists but also those of members of my other two groups, equally the volatility of the one and the indifference of the other. The problem is to discover its origins.

It is sometimes said that it is due to the decline of belief in traditional religion. I doubt very much if this is true. I do not for a moment wish to deny the importance in human history of this tendency, both as regards thought and manners. But I do not think it has much to do with the troubles of the contemporary young. The conceptions of the nature of the physical universe or of the descent and destiny of man which underlie Biblical literature, or indeed that of any of the historical world religions, ceased to be plausible to many quite a long time ago; and while this may have been slow to penetrate to the unreflecting, it cannot have been hidden from many generations of intelligent youth long before the present age. Of course, it can be argued that if we all believed that everything that happens, however deplorable, is, in some mysterious way, the fulfilment of an omnipotent, omniscient, and essentially benevolent Will, many current perplexities and anxieties would be allayed – indeed not only among the young. But this is not to say that these perplexities and anxieties are *positively caused* by the mere absence of such beliefs. That would be altogether too easy.

Much more important, I am sure, is the general erosion of belief in what may be called the liberal values. I do not think that the average member of advanced western society actually behaves with less regard to the ultimate decencies than his predecessor 50 years ago: on the contrary, I fancy I detect in many connections an amelioration of manners which is in itself admirable. But belief in the institutional framework and the social system which has fostered such changes has diminished. There is hardly any civic virtue or liberal institution which has not been subject to the acid of doubt especially among outstanding *literateurs*; and the confusion of thought which has resulted has unquestionably bred a certain infirmity of purpose. Too often it is only the gutter ideologies which are held with any great tenacity nowadays.

Nevertheless, I do not hold this to be the main cause of the malaise. A period of confusion of thought is a challenge to bold spirits; I should not expect it to evoke the moods of frustration and hopelessness which are the more disquieting features of much contemporary youthful psychology. To discover the causes of these we must look rather to the general insecurity of the future and the sense of almost complete impotence to do anything about it. It is here, in my judgement, that there are to be found the ultimate roots of the current disquiet among the more sensitive and intelligent young people of goodwill.

But is this so irrational? Are they not right in feeling that the prospects of the future are infinitely more precarious than ever before in history? No doubt many of us come to learn to live with the menaces hanging over us; it is necessary to be a little insensitive to maintain sanity in this respect. And so far as the young are concerned, I doubt if they are thinking about the ultimate possibilities every day. But the possibilities are there: and deep down they give an impermanence and an insecurity to the general outlook which colours the whole of their lives. No doubt there has always been some tendency among the more emotional to see in contemporary dangers an ultimate threat to the future. The difference in this respect between this and former ages is that *then* it was possible to argue that most of these apprehensions were baseless – that after all civilised life was likely to persist – whereas *today*, if we are honest, we can give no such confident assurance. Has there ever been a period in the world's history which has witnessed a greater aggregate of injustice and horror than the last half-century – the fratricidal slaughter of the nations of the West, the murderous tyrannies of the dictatorships both of the Right and the Left, the general collapse of international order? *Pendant que ça dure*: that surely is the secret assumption on which most of us of whatever age are tempted to act today. Can we really blame the less emotionally hardened if they are harrowed and distracted by the spectacle?

Are they to be blamed any the more if, faced with these potentialities and prospects, they are affected with a desolating sense of impotence. What assurance can we truthfully give them that those in control of events are in any sense equal to the occasion? Think calmly of reports of any meeting of the assembly of the United Nations – the organ which it was hoped would guard us from these dangers – with the dozens of splinter-state representatives frothing away in futile self-importance, all significant discussion blocked by an absence of effective power to enforce anything really significant. Think of the quality of the average oratory in a democratically elected political assembly – the empty clichés, the misleading generalities, the appeals to the gallery, the utter fourth-rateness of most of it. We, who have lived longer, know, perhaps, how to ignore or to tolerate all this – the majority of the orators are not such bad chaps after all. But who are we to condemn the more sensitive and candid who find it almost an ultimate betrayal of all to which they have been taught to attach value?

Thus in the last analysis I find the causes of a tendency to unrest among the young to be causes which should cause distress to us all. Indeed, if we of the senior generation are not distressed and apprehensive, this is surely yet another vindication of the Shavian aphorism that every man over 40 is a scoundrel.

All this is no justification for failing to deal with violence or incitements to violence, or failing to attempt to maintain decent order in teaching and the advancement of learning. But it may explain some of the difficulties besetting academic administrators in recent years.

Yours etc.

9 Staff Questions

My dear X,

Your most recent letter raises questions relating to the position of staff in higher education. What do I think has been the effect of expansion on the academic quality of staff? How do I view the alleged conflict between the claims of teaching and research? What is there to say in defence of the quite exceptional conditions of tenure and freedom in universities? Where do I stand on the question of part-time academic employment? These are serious questions demanding serious answers. In the last analysis the success or failure of academic institutions depends on the quality and disposition of the staff. A good staff with a firm grasp of the purposes for which institutions of higher education exist and the conditions essential for the performance of such purposes, may not be able to prevent occasional outbreaks of the kind of trouble I discussed in my last letter. In the confused atmosphere of the times in which we live, that would be asking for the impossible. But it can guarantee eventual survival. An institution comprising a sufficient number of teachers who are confident in their knowledge of the traditions of academic freedom and prepared to defend them is likely to survive whatever the initial onset. An institution which has not this strength is in very grave danger indeed.

First let me say a word on the effects of expansion. At the time of the publication of the Report of the Committee on Higher Education some fears were expressed concerning the maintenance of intellectual quality among a greatly increased staff. I remember cogently argued views to this effect by Professor R. V. Jones who certainly is entitled to be heard with respect in such connections.

In fact, in so far as I am capable of judgement; which, needless to say, has considerable limitations – I doubt whether these fears have proved to have been justified. It is probably true that, in a few subjects which have suddenly become widely popular, the output of trained personnel from the few existing sources was insufficient; and, in consequence some appointments were made which may have involved a lowering of quality. But, if one is to judge from the output of the learned journals, these instances are the exception rather than the rule. On the whole I suspect that the main result of the increases of demand for senior appointments was a diminution of the average age of the professoriate due to younger men getting their chance at an earlier stage – not at all a bad thing in a profession which, for reasons I will discuss later, tends to be cluttered up with a certain amount of burnt-out talent at an advanced age. It is true that, as time goes on, this phalanx of erstwhile bright young men will themselves be something of a problem, a solid obstacle to the promotion of juniors, like the dowager in the *Midsummer Night's Dream*,

> 'Long lingering out a young man's revenue'

But that is a problem of the future and not a fulfilment of the fears of rapid expansion.

There has been, however, a complication attending expansion which I fancy was not widely foreseen. The rapidity of recruitment of junior staff meant that although the majority of the recruits were by no means intellectually inferior academically to preceding generations, some of them at least were far less qualified in other ways, particularly in knowledge of the essential disciplines and wider purposes of universities. Indeed, unless special steps were taken to make good this deficiency, it might be said that some at least of them were little better informed on matters of this sort than the students they had to teach. I certainly failed to anticipate this development: a bad lack of imagination of which I am now somewhat ashamed. I hasten to add that, if I had had more foresight, it would not have shaken my belief in the desirability of expansion. It would, however, have led me explicitly to draw attention to the desirability of special measures to offset this complicating circumstance. I fancy that the worst effects have now worn off. But, as I said when discussing the induction of junior staff as one of the problems of increased size, it is certainly a matter which demands continuing vigilance.

There is, however, a much deeper problem than this; a problem which, if it is not solved successfully, may indeed cut at the roots of university expansion, the problem, namely, of the appropriate relationship between teaching and research. As we have agreed, it is the peculiar function of universities as they have developed in this country, both to hand down existing knowledge and methods of acquiring it and to contribute to its advancement. I have argued already that there are great advantages in this combination. But, at the present, there are great difficulties in preserving the right proportions.

I do not think that these difficulties were so obvious earlier on. I recollect that when I was a young don at Oxford, I once went for a walk with a distinguished senior who intimated to me that publication at an early stage might be regarded as a sign of superficiality and indeed exhibitionism. But on the whole I think that this was an untypical attitude. My impression is that in the much smaller university population of those days there was something like an appropriate balance. There were those whose major instincts tended to research and publication, and there were those whose impulses tended much more to exposition and the care of students. I wouldn't say that the state of affairs was ideal in that respect: there were some departments where research lagged and exposition was more or less static; others where research may have been overdone to the neglect of teaching; and I think it was a general deficiency of the system in those days, in this country, that there was a lack of organisation at the graduate level. But for good or bad, the balance about which I am writing would not have been regarded as a major problem.

In recent years, it seems to me that the position has changed. Both as regards the probationary period and later on, the emphasis in many universities has shifted quite definitely in favour of research and publication; at any rate, so far as establishment and promotion are concerned. I wouldn't say that things are as bad here as they appear to be in some parts of the United States where frequent publication is almost as necessary as a trade union ticket in a closed shop. But I think it is bad enough to be disturbing. How many intelligent young academics have reflected, 'What shall I do? I would like to put more into my teaching, But it is quite obvious that unless I publish more, I may not get a permanent job, let alone ultimate promotion'.

Two serious consequences follow from this state of affairs. The first, the lesser evil, is that a good deal of time is wasted on research and publication which frankly is not worthwhile. The impulse is factitious and the result insignificant. It seems to me something of a scandal that production of such a non-spontaneous nature should weigh so heavily, as distinct from successful teaching and supervision of students, when confirmation of probation is considered. Nor do I think that forcing the pace in this way is in the true interests of scholarship and the advancement of knowledge. In many subjects, at least on the humanistic side, some of the most eminent scholars have published little or nothing before reaching the age of 35 or over. I cannot believe that their performance would have been superior if the fear of termination of their appointment on the ground of insufficient publication had been hanging over their heads.

There is furthermore a second consequence even more serious than this. Where promotion depends on publication, students and teaching tend to be neglected. Teaching and supervision tend to be regarded as evils subtracting time from one's own research. I have even heard of one famous institution abroad where the teachers removed their names from their doors in order that they might not be disturbed. This seems to me a fantastically perverse state of affairs. Even if one's native inclinations are towards research rather than teaching, there are very few of us so brilliant in this respect that we may claim exemption from the immense obligations in regard to students which membership of a university involves; and, where there is such exemption, for which in large institutions with extensive division of labour there may occasionally be genuine justification, it should be by way of decision by competent authority rather than something to be sought as a result of the routine establishment and promotion requirements.

Needless to say such attitudes are perceived by the students. I personally am inclined to think that the contemporary undergraduate, inspired by nostalgic aspiration for what he calls *the* tutorial system – a one-to-one relationship which is tending to die out even where it was at one time practised, – is inclined to demand too much by way of supervision: part at any rate of the value of a period at a university is learning to teach oneself. But the sense of being not wanted, an encumbrance to be borne in order to provide funds to support research and publication on occasions when some supervision is not only desirable but essential, is not unnaturally resented. I have little doubt that some of the unrest in some contemporary universities derives from an awareness of such attitudes.

In saying all this, I am not in the least denying the importance of research and publication as essential functions of university institutions, both as contributing to the advancement of knowledge and generally as essential to the atmosphere of a university. I seek only to deprecate excessive attention to such functions to the neglect of others equally essential. The standing of a university is to be measured not only by the numbers of Fellows of the Royal Society or the British Academy on its staff, significant though that may be, but also by the efficiency of its training and stimulation of its students, both at the undergraduate and graduate levels. And who shall say who contributes most to the atmosphere of a university-a scientist or scholar who achieves international fame by his research and publications or the teacher who, keeping himself abreast of the advancement of knowledge in his range of subjects, passes on to his students his critical interest in these subjects and his general sense of dedication?

I personally think that it would be a good thing if a higher proportion of senior posts, including chairs, than prevails at present were to go to the latter type, not to mention those who are prepared to devote at least part of their time to the onerous and delicate tasks of senior departmental administration.

This brings me to the most difficult of your questions, the proliferation of the exceptional conditions of tenure and freedom enjoyed by academics, conditions superior in many ways to those enjoyed in any other profession.

Let me deal first with tenure. You will of course be aware that, before this privilege is granted for junior appointments, there are usually some probationary years. Even in the case of chairs, some such preliminary period of testing may be required. After such periods have elapsed, however, if the person concerned has satisfied requirements, he is appointed at least until the first retiring age of 62 and, since advantage is seldom taken of termination at that point by the employing authority concerned, the granting of tenure amounts *de facto* until the so-called final retiring age at 67. I ought to add that such assurances of continuing employment do not involve the process of automatic promotion. It is therefore only in the case of full professors that tenure exists without any accompanying pecuniary incentive.

Now the world at large is apt to regard this as an anomaly; and I do not think that academics should be unaware of the substantial grounds for this attitude. Needless to say there are very many academics for whom the pecuniary incentive is of minor importance, academics who go on providing contributions to knowledge and inspiration to students and their colleagues long after any pecuniary incentives have ceased to operate. But there are others who are not so motivated and whose activities in one way or another fall off once they have reached the top of the tree. Moreover different academics like members of other occupations, tend to age differently: some go on long past the retiring age, others palpably do not. The result of all this is that, in the upper reaches at least, the profession has a larger proportion than elsewhere of partially or wholly tired intellects, more or less guaranteed a position until the second retiring age and incidentally occupying posts which could be better filled by younger men. This bewilders the outside world. And it is no answer that it would be impossible to attract first-class personalities into the profession unless they were attracted by these privileges, for it is clear that, at other times and in other places, first-class people have been attracted by contracts less advantageous in respect of length and custom of tenure; and if some were deterred by limitations in this respect, it is not at all difficult to think of pecuniary adjustments which might well be at once a compensation to the persons concerned for this limitation and an advantage to the general quality of the staff.

The justification for some degree of security of tenure lies in quite another direction than the general attractiveness of the job. It lies in considerations of academic freedom, that is to say in security from dismissal for reasons of disagreement with the content of the writing or lecturing of the person concerned. I can well believe that, at certain times and in certain places, this may have been very important; and although I very much doubt that in the United Kingdom at least, *external* pressures of this kind would go very far nowadays or arise very often, I can easily conceive of *internal* pressures, from politically-minded staff and students *of either extreme*, which might easily become a menace, even if it might be invidious to quote contemporary examples.

For this reason I personally think that there is still a valid case for some tenure. But I cannot believe that it is not overdone with present arrangements and dispositions. I myself, in more than half a century's acquaintance with academic life, have never seen the appointment of any professor terminated on academic grounds at the first retiring age – two years longer than the retiring age of first-class public servants – although I could certainly name, though I do not intend to do so, cases where such retirement would have been abundantly justified. Academic committees are notoriously generous in such cases, even where a falling off of quality is conspicuous.

'Poor old Y, he has borne the burden and heat of the day. Moreover if we carry him on for another five years his pension will be that much higher'. I should be interested to learn of cases where such arguments have not prevailed.

I should therefore regard it as a prime essential of maintaining our credentials *vis-à-vis* not only the Philistine, but also the reflective public, that the first retiring age, if not actually lowered to that of the public service, should be made the subject of less nominal and more serious consideration: I would urge moreover that the onus of proof should be, not that the prolongation of Y to the second retiring age will not do much harm, but *rather that it is preferable to any other arrangement*. I need hardly say that such a policy would justifiably necessitate considerable adjustment of conditions regarding pensions. A man should not be penalised for retiring at the earlier age. Doubtless this might involve costs. But they need not be considerable in relation to salary and pension arrangements in general; and they would be a small price to pay for elbow-room to cut out dead wood – though I do not think that that is how the change need be regarded. It is really not a disgrace for the presumption to be that retirement should be usual at roughly speaking the same age as that of first-class public servants; and retirement from full-time responsibility need not preclude part-time continuation, on a year to year basis, for many years thereafter. With such arrangements in vogue, if a man really loves his subject and continues to be competent to teach it, the deprivation of the panoply and power of a full-time chair need not involve any justifiable feeling of being unappreciated or discarded.

But what about academic freedom itself you may ask. Does not my argument imply that to set such store by it I am prepared to sacrifice controls which, in any other walk of life, would be regarded as indispensable. Does it not mean, backed up by tenure, freedom for academics to do exactly what they like and freedom to ignore all sorts of things that other people would regard as duties?

With respect, this interpretation is not valid. Let me begin by making clear what in my conception academic freedom does not imply.

First it does not imply freedom to neglect the duties which are implied in one's contract, namely to teach in a certain field, to accept one's part in a common programme of lectures, not to be absent without leave or to refuse to supervise students which are allotted to one. Whether such obligations are spelt out in so many words, no one of good sense would hold that it was an infringement of academic freedom to enforce them if they were neglected.

Secondly it does not involve action or exhortation to disturb the decent order of the institution by which one is employed. Doubtless there is scope here for disagreement about measures conducive to decent order; and it would certainly be quite wrong to inhibit freedom of discussion in this respect. But any participation in violence or encouragement thereof obviously oversteps these limits; and the academic who feels impelled to act in this way, whatever the sincerity of his convictions, is certainly not justified in appealing to the principles of academic freedom in his defence.

The essence of academic freedom is liberty as regards the communication of thought relevant to the subjects assigned by contract. Given the subject he is engaged to teach, the academic should be free to teach it the way he thinks appropriate and to impart what he believes to be the truth about the questions he discusses. No tradition of orthodox interpretation should inhibit his teaching what he believes to be correct. No deference to the views of colleagues or superiors should interfere with his expression of his own conviction. This does not mean that, if he is assigned to lecture about climate, he is free to turn that course into an exposition of sociology or, if he is engaged as a mathematician, he may spend his official time expatiating upon the history of ethics. It does mean, however, that, within the field for which his contract holds, he is not bound by any intellectual consideration other than his own conviction of what is right.

Now it is clear that this degree of freedom is liable to abuses. It may be made the vehicle for the systematic inculcation of a party line – even a party line itself inimical to academic freedom. In a very temperate monograph which has evoked very intemperate denunciation, Professor Julius Gould has drawn attention to systematic abuses of this kind; and I have no doubt that his examples are true and disturbing. A teacher in social work who attributes diseases, such as insanity, to the nature of the social system, must either be so naïve as not to be fitted to be a teacher or conducting propaganda inappropriate to a university. And the examination paper which Professor Gould reproduces – for obvious reasons not mentioning its source – seems a dubious feature of any institution claiming to give an *academic* treatment of the subject that it deals with. Anyone who believes that there is not a certain amount of this insidious sort of thing prevalent in our universities at the present time, is peculiarly liable to self-deception.

The trouble is to know how to deal with it. It is an obvious platitude that in the last analysis, the principles of liberty do not oblige us to tolerate the enemies of liberty. But this is no clear guide in dealing with individual cases. It would be an uncivilised and indeed an absurd thing to deny academic appointment to all those who, on conscientious grounds, refused to denounce the operation centuries ago of the medieval inquisition. It would not, however, be uncivilised or absurd to eschew the claims of one, however otherwise distinguished, who indulged in public propaganda for the revival of such practices. Doubtless much can be done in this connection by reasonable inquiry before appointment is made – the principles of academic freedom do not exclude a minimum of worldly wisdom. The great perplexity arises when the sinister propagandist urge begins to manifest itself only when probation has ended and tenure has been granted. Here, the advocacy of violence apart, my own judgement would be in favour of tolerating the *status quo* in spite of its inconveniences. The line between what is legitimate expression of sincerely held opinion and participation in dubious propaganda is so difficult to draw that I should be inclined to put up with the consequences of past mistakes, rather than run the risk of impairing the application of the general principles of academic freedom. But that is not to say that the flagrant cases have anything to grumble about if their tendencies are dragged into the open for public appraisal as in Professor Gould's very valuable contribution.

As for definite political affiliations, I myself, as an economist dealing with subjects which have almost always a political penumbra, have always regarded it as more prudent explicitly to avoid connection with any party and to seek to judge any question which may attract my professional attention on my conviction of its merits according to my own private beliefs; in the Second Chamber I have always listened and voted as a cross-bencher. But I hasten to say that I do not regard such abstention as incumbent on academic colleagues. A man may be deeply involved in politics and yet be a good academic teacher – if anyone has any doubt of this, let him read the account given in my *Autobiography* of the late Lord Dalton as a teacher at the London School of Economics. The fundamental principle for academics, when dealing with controversial subjects, is to explain explicitly that they are controversial and, if one is conscious of bias in one direction or another, to say so candidly and so to put one's hearers on guard. It is deadening to regard matters of controversy as taboo in teaching; but it is misleading to students not to indicate their nature.

Finally you raise the question of the employment in universities of part-timers. Here, according to the principle I have just laid down, I must declare my bias, for after a long period of full-time employment I have myself become a part-timer; and, as I have related in my *Autobiography*, I was involved in what at the time was a somewhat painful dispute with a majority of the Senate of the University of London concerning my eligibility for this status.

Having made this clear, let me say that I think that universities in this country, in comparison with many universities abroad, have suffered some deprivation by so little use of the part-time employment of experts in academic subjects whose principal employment is elsewhere. Such arrangements, in my observation, have a twofold advantage. So far as the universities are concerned, they afford a wider field of recruitment and, at the same time, involve a more intimate connection with various branches of outside activity. At the same time, so far as business and other forms of professional expertise are concerned, they afford access to techniques and methods of understanding otherwise not continuously accessible. On both sides I think there arises advantage to society.

Contemporary prejudice in this country against such connections, in so far as it does not relate simply to a desire to keep narrow the market, arises mainly from unfortunate experience in medical faculties, the one branch of university activity where it has been widely practised. Here I have no doubt that, at one time, it was overdone, in that teaching depended almost entirely on distinguished outsiders and there were far too few permanent senior appointments to maintain coherence of programmes and methods of instruction. This led to unfortunate results and doubtless needed correction. But the fact that an otherwise good thing is carried too far is no argument for its total, or virtually total, rejection.

In this connection I well remember a conversation on this matter with the distinguished head of the Department of Electrical Engineering at one of the great technological universities in Europe. I asked him what he thought of part-time employment. 'Well,' he said, 'I think that at one time we relied too much on that sort of thing. But I think we have now got it more or less right'. I pressed him for more precision as regards proportions. 'Oh about fifty-fifty' was the answer. It did not surprise me that both his department and the great company from which he drew many of his part-time assistants were among the most famous of their kind in Europe. And while I should hesitate to recommend, in respect to other branches of knowledge, anything like the proportion which he regarded as about right, I am in no doubt at all of the advantage which many continental societies have gained by the more intimate connection between the universities and the outside world which the employment of suitable part-timers involves.

Yours etc.

10 The Government of Universities

My dear X,

My very sketchy answers to your questions about staff privileges and duties in universities have prompted you to inquire concerning the structure of government of such bodies – who controls whom, where initiative lies and what body is responsible for interpretation of the constitution and accountability for finance. This is the most difficult question you have yet posed, partly because university constitutions differ, at any rate in detail, so the precise answers to general questions are apt to be misleading; partly because matters of initiative and responsibility are usually so widely diffused that simple description even of any one university or university college is liable to distort the subtleties of interdependence. All that I can do, therefore, without departing from the informality of our correspondence, is to pick out salient questions of policy relating to the different functions involved and to discuss them in a broad way which I hope will be more or less generally applicable. I ought, however, to say at once that the degree of applicability will be very attenuated as regards Oxford and Cambridge because of their unique historical constitutions, and that it has no necessary connection at all with the vast variety of university institutions abroad.

Let me begin by a few observations on the effective head of a typical university, or large university college, the Vice-Chancellor, Principal, Director, Provost or by whatever other designation he is called.

I think it would be generally agreed among those who have had the responsibility of making such appointments, that of all posts connected with university life, this is easily the most difficult to fill nowadays. At earlier periods of which I have no intimate personal experience, this may have been otherwise. The number of vacancies was smaller and the duties were less extensive; and the number of

competent persons who were willing to be considered as candidates
was proportionally greater. But, with the increase in the number of
university institutions, and the multiplication of administrative
functions, the range of suitable and willing candidates is proportionately less. Happy the governing body – and I was chairman
of such a one – which is unanimous as regards what it wants and is
successful first time in its approaches. I personally do not think that
the number of persons who would be competent to discharge the
necessary functions has proportionately diminished. But I do think
that the burdens are so much greater and the increase in
emoluments has been so much less, that fewer persons of the
requisite qualifications are available for short-listing. In my opinion
we do not pay vice-chancellors enough.

What are these qualifications? It goes without saying that they
must include administrative ability in a wide range of connections.
But they must also include ability to decentralise. A vice-chancellor
who clutters himself up with extensive administrative detail will not
have enough time to do the things which he and he alone can do
properly, namely the external representation of his institution, the
maintenance of quality in senior appointments and, generally
speaking, leadership in the evolution of the broader aspects of
academic policy.

I do not think it is necessary that the vice-chancellor should have
been an academic, in the sense that he himself has made important
contributions to the advancement of knowledge or has been
outstanding as a teacher though, if such a qualification be combined
with administrative ability and the capacity to handle difficult
people, as it sometimes is, it is a very fortunate circumstance. But it
certainly is an indispensible qualification that he should have a deep
understanding of the academic function, both as regards teaching
and research. The best administrator in the world will fail in this
particular context if he is defective in this respect. The academics
should have no justification for looking down upon him as regards
this kind of insight; and he himself should not feel that, because of his
different background, he has any reserves about the uninhibited
discharge of this part of his duties.

It would be a great mistake to conceive of the vice-chancellor as a
dictator. The ultimate responsibility for what goes on rests with the
governing body, usually called the Court, and the committees to
which it devolves its powers, about which there will be more to say
later; and the vice-chancellor and his administrative subordinates

are subject to its decisions. Also, while he is chairman of the bodies responsible to the Court for recommendations regarding academic policy and discipline, he must pass on to the governing body resolutions emanating from such bodies, even if he disagrees with them. But, if he is equal to his job, he is nevertheless in a very strong position. The governing body is unlikely to impose on him decisions which he finds unpalatable. And, if he is in disagreement with his academic affairs which are virtually self-governing at some point or recommendations, he will be unable to give them his ultimate support.

I now come to the conduct of academic policy. Again in the last resort this is the responsibility of the governing body. But it has long been a convention that, save in regard to matters involving major financial changes or administrative arrangements, academic business is left to the academics. Of course one can think of lunatic developments, say in the sense of members of a particular department pledging themselves to the exclusive service of some particular business or political party, where the governing body would have a duty to step in. But such possibilities are so remote that I only mention them to emphasise the contrast with the tradition of academic affairs which are virtually self-governing at some point or other.

We may begin with the work of individual departments. Here obviously where there is more than one teacher concerned there must be some allocation of duties. If the department is a small one this is obviously the responsibility of the professor in charge. If there is more than one professor, there must be some committee with a chairman. In either case, if any of the junior teachers considers himself or herself over-loaded or in other ways unjustly treated, there should be the right to appeal to the vice-chancellor or someone delegated by him or by the Academic Board, of which more later. On the whole there should be little compulsion here. It is a very unwise head of a department who is not in frequent consultation with his juniors. But this is not to say that such unwisdom does not exist; and it is part of the business of superior bodies to reduce it to a minimum.

We may next notice the organisation of courses interrelated by subject matter or by the requirements of examinations. These are concerned with curricula, the appointment of boards of examiners and the prescription of common standards; and it is certainly appropriate that not only senior teachers but juniors, at least those having tenure, should be represented on them. The allocation of duties within departments is a function which needs to be supported by a spot of authority. But where it is a question of standards and scope in the wide sense, there is no monopoly of wisdom in the professoriate; and a professor who wishes to impose his point of view must do so in virtue of superior argumentative power and general standing rather than in virtue of his position in the hierarchy. A distinction is sometimes made in the United Kingdom between boards of studies dealing with particular subjects and faculties dealing with wide groups of interrelated subjects – in the United States it should be noted the term faculty relates to the entire academic body. But this is not necessarily the most suitable grouping, especially for the arrangement of courses and examinations appropriate to broad degrees: and my own opinion is that the faculty as such, in the UK sense, has now very limited utility. I would only add that, where graduate studies form a sizable proportion of the activities of the university as a whole, a special committee is necessary to deal with questions of admission standards, the authorisation of subjects and the arrangement of supervision of researches which overlap the province of more than one department.

We now come to the chief academic body which exists to discuss the widest questions of standards, scope, discipline and external relations and, with one exception which I will dwell upon shortly, to make authoritative recommendations to the governing body.

Here the main problem is size. I can see no reason of principle for excluding from voting power any teacher whose tenure has been confirmed, and I think that there is a case for representation by proper election of those teachers who are not in that position, though I do not think that injustice is done by exclusion of those who are not so elected. But even with this limitation, which no longer prevails in some universities, there are real difficulties in excessive numbers. Every candid person of experience of such bodies will admit that the probability of intimate and candid talk on the various questions which arise diminishes markedly as a board becomes a large meeting. There is a double danger here. First the temptation to emotional rhetoric which, as all the world knows, grows rapidly with the size of the audience. Secondly there is the danger – a very real one in my experience – that many of the most serious-minded members of the staff will absent themselves just for the reason that they regard it as a waste of time to attend that 'talking shop'. This is doubtless understandable. But it is none the less deplorable and must in the end erode the excellence of the evolution of policy unless something is done about it.

As I see things, the only available remedy is a strong general purposes committee whose size, although representative, can be so limited as to be conducive to sober and candid conversation. A committee of this sort, although obliged to report its recommendations can, if suitably chaired, establish a relationship of trust, such that, save on matters of really momentous importance, the proceedings of the main board can be limited so as to be tolerable to most serious-minded persons. But it would be self-deception to believe that all problems can be settled by this device.

There is one set of problems which certainly fall into the category of the academic, which are peculiar in the sense that the academic board or its general purposes committee is not suitable to deal with them. These are the problems of promotion and appointment. Here is a sphere where the function of recommendation should be confined to the professoriate, both as regards promotion and as regards appointment, at any rate at the senior levels. The reason for this belief is certainly not any strong conviction on my part that professors as such are necessarily intellectually superior to other members of the staff: quite the contrary, indeed, as I have indicated already in another connection; I can conceive that a certain proportion of the professoriate take life rather more easily once that position has been reached. *The reason is rather that in this respect they have no further to go* and, to that extent therefore, have no temptation to think of what the effect on their own position may be, if they vote for one person rather than one another. This is not to say that, in all sorts of indirect ways, they may not be influenced by considerations other than the relative standing and suitability for the duties involved of the candidates under discussion. That assumption would fit only a community of archangels. But it is to say as regards promotion and appointments that, being without hope themselves as regards further advancement, they are immune from temptation to form alliances the substance of which is mutual assistance in this connection. To say this is not to say that there are not very many members of the non-professoriate grades who would not regard with extreme distaste any intrigues of this sort. It is to say, however, that the temptation might exist, and that the limitation for which I am arguing prevents it being operative.

There is a further need at least so far as the most senior

appointments are concerned, namely the need that the range of external advice should be widened. This means, firstly, that at least one lay member of the governing body should be a member of the board of electors, and secondly that external experts from other universities should be members – an admirable practice which, here as in examinations both at the undergraduate and graduate level, has done much to sustain substantial uniformity of minimum levels in most subjects. I need hardly say that, in addition to these safeguards, the governing body itself should have an opportunity of reviewing the recommendations finally before they are confirmed, though it must be a rare occasion for nominations reached on this expert and detached level to be called in question.

This brings me at last to the governing body itself. Practice in this respect varies widely. Some Courts are very large – the Committee on Higher Education discovered cases where numbers ran into hundreds – some are much smaller. In the former class recruitment has obviously been based on the desire to enlist support of various kinds rather than continuous supervision – a motive not to be frivolously derided. But where numbers are large, it is essential that active powers should be delegated to a smaller executive committee, meeting frequently and capable of frank and confidential discussion, with meetings of the full Court taking place perhaps twice or three times a year to receive reports and to deliberate on matters which the executive decides deserve wider ventilation.

It should be clear that the composition of the executive body is a matter of great importance. At one time academic representation tended to be outnumbered by lay members. In recent years, rightly in my opinion, this unbalance has tended to be remedied. The chairman should be a layman in the sense that, even if he takes part in lectures and seminars, he is not in any way a member of the full-time academic staff. But, provided that he has a casting vote in the unlikely event of all the lay members being of one view and all the academics of another, I see no objection to equality on this body between lay and academic representation. It means that academic decisions are made with adequate academic advice and it maintains adequate continuity of relationship between the active laymen and the various academic boards and committees. In my own experience of such a body, it was never divided on representational lines.

It is sometimes argued that in our day the lay element is superfluous, a residue of the past and an unwarranted intrusion of inexpert knowledge in the conduct of academic institutions. This view seems to me to be ill-founded both substantially and as a matter of practical wisdom. Substantially it is just not true that active lay governors have little to contribute to the running of universities. Universities do not function in a vacuum: they have external problems as well as problems which are peculiar to their internal business and the two sets of problems are often interrelated. No one with experience of the part which lay governors have played in the foundation and continuous business of running universities can have any doubt of the contribution which they are able to make. But, quite apart from this, as a matter of practical wisdom, it is simply not to be believed that, at the present day, modern universities which are heavily subsidised by the state, should be given large sums of money without intimate guarantees that these are responsibly spent. It is true that, in this respect, the ancient universities of Oxford and Cambridge have no laymen on their governing bodies. In the judgement of many they suffer in various ways from this deficiency. But whether that is true or not, it is quite unbelievable that other, more recently founded, universities should enjoy similar immunity. For the rest of us, the choice is between much closer control by organs of the state or some element of lay control in their constitution. Those who have personal acquaintance with universities abroad where state control is direct, will have no difficulty in deciding which system is preferable. And even if it is arguable that means of state control can be devised which are not so authoritarian as systems abroad – and no one will deny that we have achievements in this connection – it is not reasonable to suppose that any amount of ingenuity could devise anything so flexible and adaptable as the decentralised management by lay and academic elements which exists in most universities in Britain today.

I have left to the last the most contentious question – the extent to which students as such should participate in the business of the government of universities. I have touched on this question when I wrote to you on the nature and causes of student militancy and unrest. But propaganda for student participation in the government of universities has been very fashionable in the last few years; and since I think it has led to harmful conceptions of policy in some instances and the almost incredible waste of the time needed for the performance of essential services, I think it is worthwhile expatiating on it at some length in this context.

The movement for student power, the demand for the control or partial control by students of university institutions, assumes two forms which we may call, respectively, the anti-rational and the rational. The one demands power as an end in itself, regardless of its compatibility with the other ends of the society; the other purports to provide a justification of its demands in terms of compatibility with, or indeed benefit to, social aims in general.

The anti-rational branch of this movement has much in common with the more extreme forms of the Syndicalist movement which flourished in Europe at the beginning of the century and which finds its classic formulation in the *Reflections on Violence* of George Sorel, a work which in its day enjoyed a sort of snob prestige as an alleged liquidator of all traditional values. When it does not consist of a mere affirmation – 'We want power and we mean to have it' – it is essentially an expression of contempt for or disgust at existing institutions. Democracy has failed – look at the present state of affairs. The existing structure of society is hateful. There is no hope of change through the normal channels of politics. There is nothing for it but for groups of dedicated persons to capture certain islands of possible autonomy; and, obliterating all traces of an ignoble past, to govern them according to the hearts' desire of the progressive and enlightened spirits who have emerged triumphant from the struggle. It is essentially a defiance of a coordinated society.

Conceived in this spirit, the prospects of student power are not very hopeful. The prospects of extreme syndicalism never were. The intellectual *coup de grâce* indeed was administered long ago by the alleged wisecrack of the Webbs – the sewers for the sewage men. Where, as in the United Kingdom, the majority of the students receive not only their fees but also their day to day maintenance from the central government or the local authorities, the claim that they should operate the institutions intended for their instruction, without any control from teachers or the outside world, is not likely to command wide acceptability. One need only talk to waiters in the canteens or the uniformed attendants in institutions where there has been extremist trouble, to discover how hated this kind of thing is to the people who have actually come up the hard way. And since the rebels are a minority – and indeed, as I have argued earlier, a small minority even of the student body – there can be little doubt that this sort of agitation will eventually produce a reaction.

Confronted with this brute fact, the majority of such groups – apart from the extreme extremists – are usually prepared to beat a strategic retreat into the camp of those who are prepared to use reason and persuasion, and who base their demand for student control or extensive student representation not on wild nihilist gestures but upon arguments designed to show that social interest and social equity would be best secured thereby. And since, in my judgement, there is at least an infusion of cogency in some of these arguments, they certainly need examining further.

Let me say at once what I have emphasised already that I recognise justice and utility in the claim that students should be consulted in some way or other in matters in which their convenience and interests are clearly concerned, university administrators and governing bodies are not omniscient; and there arise continually positions in which their regulations and directives may cause needless inconvenience or even hardship to students. There is thus everything to be said for forms of organisation which permit student opinion on such matters to be regularly ventilated, rather than leaving its emergence to chance conversation or *ad hoc* demonstrations against particular grievances. Where university authorities resist the establishment of any organisation of this sort, they have only themselves to thank if the reaction of impetuous and high-spirited youth sometimes takes an ugly form.

How exactly such organisations should be constituted is a matter about which opinions may differ and in regard to which local tradition and social custom may well play a determining part. The obvious form is representative committees concerned with the administrative functions bearing directly upon student welfare – library committees, refectory committees, entertainment committees and so on – taking for granted a good deal of student autonomy in regard to sport and athletics. But if it serves to reassure the student body that the more general aspects of policy are considered with due regard to their welfare, I see no objection in principle to some limited membership, on a suitably-devised franchise, on the general Court of Governors, always subject to the reservation that this does not involve membership of its executive committee whose composition I have discussed at an earlier stage.

Beyond this, I see grave difficulties. The idea that the effective functioning of universities as such, the appointment of academic staff and officers, the devising of courses, the setting of standards, the advancement of knowledge, are likely to be benefited by student control does not seem to me plausible. On the contrary, I see grave dangers to the very purposes for which universities are founded; and although always anxious to proceed by persuasion rather than coercion, in the end I should be prepared to resist such proposals without concessions.

Why is this? I examine my conscience carefully in this respect and I am clear enough that it does not arise from any feelings of antagonism or superiority to students in general. Personally, I love the company of students and find their outlook often considerably more congenial than that of some of my colleagues. But, on fundamental matters of this sort, I take what may be called a functional view of desirable educational organisations. And, as I see things, judgements on the suitability of appointments, the curricula of degree courses and examination requirements, are not among the functions which students, *as students*, are fitted to perform. If they were, if they were competent to gauge academic quality or to determine the desiderata of various branches of knowledge, they would not be students; they would already have the competence which would make them eligible for election to the staff. There is surely everything to be said for teachers trying to discover, not only by examination and observation but also by direct inquiry, what effect is produced by their teaching and whether the tradition of examination questions is thought to be fair. But we are on the other side of the limits of the desirable if students are given constitutional rights to select teachers and administrators or to have a hand in the setting of standards.

There is a further and perhaps even deeper reason why the student body should not be admitted to powers involving this degree of control: it is fundamentally inimical to the main conception of academic freedom. If elections to chairs and the prescription of what shall and shall not be taught is to be within the power of the student body, there is critical danger here. I do not for a moment say that such powers would *necessarily* be abused. But I do say that there is plenty of evidence that their existence might very easily run the danger of the introduction of all sorts of irrelevant elements, as we have recently seen in various continental universities. And I cannot believe that conditions in which the appointment of teachers and the framing of courses were subject to student control and perhaps student agitation, would be conducive to the free development of academic traditions, either by individuals or institutions, which is so important if liberty of the intellect is to survive. The sort of student who agitates for student power is the sort of student who would readily lead a movement against a professional appointment which was disliked on political grounds. I am not in the least unaware of the dangers of academic freedom itself. It is a state of affairs which may be abused by unscrupulous academics. I am also not unaware of the fact that academics and their governing bodies may make, and that students may then suffer, mistaken appointments. But taking all this into account, I am sure that the admission of student control in this group of functions would bring with it less, rather than more, of the desirable aspects of academic freedom than we have at present.

Finally it should surely be clear that the presence of student representatives on the main decision-making bodies would inhibit efficient discussion. Let us suppose for instance that it is a matter of providing finance for competing research projects. Funds are limited and the executive committee has to make a choice. It may be that on purely academic grounds the projects are equally deserving. But the committee has to take account too of the probability of their completion. One of the applicants is thought to be more talented than the other. But against this it has been noticed by his colleagues that his work lately has been more and more intermittent, that he is more and more prone to long periods of melancholia and that his relations with those with whom he has to work have become more and more difficult. Are these matters which can be ignored by a body responsible for the wise spending of public money? Yet are they questions which can be discussed with candour in the presence of students? Obviously discussion of such immensely relevant matters would have to take place on the side. This is an imaginary example. But, as anyone who has had acquaintance with this kind of top-level decision-making must admit, it is not in the least unrealistic. Matters of parallel delicacy are likely to come up very frequently. What possible reason therefore can be adduced for creating a state of affairs in which the proceedings of the bodies titularly responsible for making such decisions are in the nature of a sham, and the real business has to be done by arts and stratagems and backstairs consultations. Quite apart from the intrinsic distastefulness of such goings on, is it not almost certain that the quality of the decisions thus reached must suffer and the efficiency, and thus eventually the utility of the university to its students be impaired?

Yours etc.

11 The State and the Universities

My dear X,

After your inquiries concerning the internal government of university institutions, you now raise the question of state control. To what extent is the government involved in this area – the area of the so-called 'autonomous' branches of higher education? What are the possible mechanisms in this respect and which, if any, is the desirable alternative? What are the principles of the existing mechanism and what is its relation to the Cabinet and to Parliament? I do not doubt that much of this is already known to you. But an outline orderly review of the main problems involved may perhaps facilitate further discussion.

Perhaps I should begin by reminding you that all universities in this country operate within a framework of law – general law regarding the behaviour of corporations, special law relating to universities as such and arising from the existence of different forms of charter. What may be done or what may not be done within this framework is quite a complicated matter; and not all lawyers are capable of dealing with it. While nowadays a vice-chancellor or any other head of institutions of higher education needs to be capable of following explanations in these terms, he would be unwise who, without very specialised training, relied on his own wits in such matters. Nor may the interpretations and judgements of the courts be easy to anticipate in this connection. There are grey areas here where almost anything can happen.

In the distant past, the ancient universities here suffered much from the interference of monarchs and governments and, in the periods of the Reformation and the Great Rebellion, were marked by intrusions in respect of religious affiliations which we should now regard as quite unbelievable – save that we have seen something of the same sort elsewhere in our own times in the interests of the new religion, Communism; and I should not be personally sure of the behaviour in this country either of a Leftist minority – not the main body of the Labour Party – or of the more aggressive elements of the so-called National Front in the, let us hope, unlikely event of either group coming into power. The upshot of all this toing and froing left Oxford and Cambridge in the position of having power to admit only persons who were prepared to subscribe to the 39 articles of the Church of England – a position which was only relaxed by the University Acts of 1871; and the position as regards the use of endowments particularly on the part of the colleges, was often disgraceful.

In the nineteenth century there were movements for reform, both within the ancient universities and through Acts of Parliament, particularly in regard to statutes and the use of money. On the whole it can be said that these were definitely in the public interest and certainly not limiting academic freedom in any undesirable way. At the same time, other universities came into being South of the Border whose statutes and degree – granting powers involved government authorisation in some shape or other. But on the whole it cannot be said that, before the present century, there was anything like a general state policy for universities in the United Kingdom; and I am sure that the problem with which you wish me to deal relates to them, rather than to past changes in the law or the shape of particular charters.

The problem relates essentially to the use of government money. It is true that, from time to time in the nineteenth century, special grants were made to special institutions; London University for instance received a small sum – £3370 in 1841 – for its general examining purposes. Later on, by 1902, the number of recipient universities was fourteen; and from 1889 onwards there were special advisory committees to advise the Treasury regarding the distribution of the very small sums involved. It was not until the present century that a combination of circumstances brought it about that a more systematic policy had to be adopted. There is an extremely good account of all this in Professor Berdahl's *British Universities and the State* (Cambridge University Press, 1959).

Before discussing in outline the solution actually adopted and the way it works, it is perhaps worthwhile looking at the various alternatives as regards policy in this respect.

The first alternative is complete abstention from subsidy. This would not mean that there would have been no universities. It must be remembered that the colleges of Oxford and Cambridge were considerable owners of real estate and the universities concerned were subsidised from part of the resulting income. There was also revenue derived from fees. Similar arrangements on a more modest but, in the eighteenth century at least, on a much more education- ally effective scale, prevailed in Scotland. In the United States some of the most distinguished universities have been founded and, sustained by private subscriptions and fees, and have established standards seldom excelled by anywhere else in the world. It is spoiling a good case to argue that, if the state were to maintain an attitude of complete detachment as regards the financing of universities, there would be *nothing* of that sort in existence.

But, according to modern ideas – to which I subscribe – it would not be enough to meet the number of applicants with adequate qualifications. In the United States, where the continued existence of institutions privately founded and supported by fees and subscriptions is conspicuous, there are also gigantic state un- iversities, some of which are equally eminent; and, without them, the high proportion of the population having had contact with universities would have been impossible. Certainly if the present area of university studies which, directly or indirectly, is supported by the state in this country, were subtracted from the whole, the university population would be most severely contracted.

Similar considerations apply to the advancement of knowledge. Here too, while we must not ignore the endowments and subscrip- tions from private or business sources – not to mention the great foundations – it is very clear that if it were not for public subsidy, this side of university activity would be a fraction of what it is today. And whatever may be thought of the global amounts devoted to research and the proportion which is worthwhile in a practical sense or as intrinsically valuable knowledge, I doubt if many knowledge- able people would view without dismay the degree of contraction which the absence of public support would involve.

Of course, if one lets one's imagination loose, it is possible to think of alternative arrangements whereby some of this contraction might be avoided. If instead of the present system of state-financed fees and grants subject only to a means test, there were a system of loans on the lines suggested by Professor Prest and discussed at some length in an earlier letter, it is possible to believe that the problem of numbers could be solved that way. And since I personally believe that the Prest scheme has advantages in many ways superior to the present system, I should not grumble at such a change. I am bound to point out, however, to any who are carried away by the arguments in favour of such arrangements that they must not exaggerate the immediate financial advantages which would accrue to the public revenue. There would be a long transition period before the Prest scheme, however elaborated, would be self-financing.

Even supposing this to come about, there remains research and the advancement of learning to be provided for. Here too it is possible to think of some mitigation of a hands-off policy. In my judgement there is much to be said for some research, at present financed from public sources, to be paid for on a customer-seller relationship of the kind so forcefully advocated by Lord Rothschild. But this does not meet the case where pure speculation or pure scholarship is involved;and although it may be argued that some additional money spent in this way could be raised from sources other than government, I do not doubt the very great damage which would be done to our universities if that part of research which does not immediately show practical and saleable results were denied public support. In my judgement that would be a cultural disaster.

Thus whatever modifications which may be thought of for the future as regards methods of finance, the conclusion is unavoidable that the modern state is involved directly or indirectly in very large support to university finances; and at present and indeed for a long time to come, that support cannot be extensively curtailed without results which would be antipathetic to most enlightened opinion. We come back therefore to our main problem. If the state is so involved, what form does such involvement take? It is obviously unthinkable that sums of the order of magnitude of hundreds of millions should be handed over to academic institutions without any control other than the presence of reputable lay members on the governing bodies, important though, as I have argued earlier, such control may be. The question is what shape that control should take.

The obvious solution and one which is adopted in many countries is that the universities should be subject to direct control by the state. If the universities are sustained in large measure by government expenditure – at one time the support here was in the neighbourhood of 85 per cent – what could be more logical than that the direction of this expenditure should be in the hands of a minister responsible to Parliament with an appropriate body of officials to manage day to day operations, with perhaps some *ad hoc* consultation with vice-chancellors and other interested bodies.

In fact, however, such a solution involves dangers – dangers which threaten the better side of university life as we have known it. I would not argue that such dangers always materialise. It would be foolish to minimise the accomplishments of universities in parts of the free world where the state has direct control, just as it would be superfluous to emphasise the deplorable state of affairs, at any rate in most, if not all, subjects prevailing in totalitarian regimes. Let me try to spell out the dangers to which modern western democracies may be exposed.

First is the danger of excessive bureaucratisation – the multiplication of minute controls, particularly financial, of institutional expenditure. A university which has to submit to some central office proposals for the switching of small funds from one object to another – the appointment of a research assistant in place of expenditure on the time of a computer, for instance – is certainly not free. And this example is not imaginary. A high official in charge of education in one of the most reputable areas of continental Europe assured me that that was the procedure in his sphere of jurisdiction. When I asked him if it did not cause occasional friction, he replied 'Never'; but a young man who was translating for certain members of the party added, behind his hand, 'because we are a set of sheep'.

A much greater danger than this, however, is the danger of what may be described as the inappropriate intrusion of politics into the business of higher education. Let me be quite clear about this. The decision to spend immense sums of money on higher education is essentially a political decision and no sensible person would wish to deny the right of ministers to lay down broad principles of policy and administration in this connection – for me politics is not always a dirty word. Whether any particular principle thus laid down is an infringement of academic liberty is a matter to be solved *ambulando*; we get nowhere by blanket prohibitions of any principle whatever. The danger arises rather one stage lower down. The evaluation of the performance of particular institutions and the allocation of funds between them is a function which, if it is to be discharged efficiently and without danger to academic freedom, needs to be done in an atmosphere from which political considerations are absent. So does the evolution of policy in regard to the development of particular disciplines. There is a real danger, if the discharge of these functions lies with organs directly involved in politics, that much irrelevance and worse may intrude and impede the emergence of objective recommendations and decisions appropriate to the real needs of the situation. There is a real danger that policies inimical to academic freedom may be adopted. I will not contend that this will necessarily happen. But I would contend that common sense and common experience unite in suggesting that it easily may happen.

Fortunately there is an alternative which, to the immense credit of some ministers of the past and their top advisors, has been evolved in this country; this alternative, to a considerable extent at any rate, avoids these dangers while preserving reasonable control of the expenditure concerned. If the state is willing to entrust the distribution of public money for this purpose and the scrutiny of the way in which it has been spent, not directly to a government department inevitably subject to political control and influence, but indirectly to a non-political expert commission or committee; and if that body, so far as is consistent with the execution of the larger aims of public policy, makes its grants in forms which impose a minimum of precise specification on the detail of expenditure, then there is created a partial insulation which should be sufficient to protect academic institutions against the cruder incursions of politics and to create an area in which freedom to maintain their own standards and initiate their own development is reasonably well preserved. It can create, too, an organisation in which whatever positive coordination and joint planning is necessary, can take place without political coercion and without as much of friction and necessary give and take which occurs between departments and faculties in a large university with a lay element in its ultimate organ of government.

I will not conceal my belief that the University Grants Committee, which embodies such practices, is one of the happiest of our constitutional inventions. Whatever may be its role in the future, it would be difficult to deny that, so far, it has operated in such a way as to permit the transmission to the universities of a large volume of public money without serious encroachment on essential academic freedoms. In the main, what criticisms can be made of the policy of higher education in this country in recent years must rest on the failure of governments at a time of financial crisis to give adequate notice of its intentions – a failure which has given rise to all sorts of frustrations and inefficiencies, rather than on any inequity in their distribution and administration. Whatever may be said from time to time at home by disappointed vice-chancellors and

professors, – who are decidedly not non-existent – there can be no
doubt of the envy and esteem in which the University Grants
Committee is held among academics and academic administrators
abroad. It is true that such arrangements are contingent on the
willingness of ministers and Parliament to tolerate them and that, in
times of great political tension, this willingness may easily be
suspended. But this is true also of many other arrangements which
in normal times are an adequate safeguard of various individual and
institutional freedoms. The fact that they do not provide a 100 per
cent guarantee is no reason for denying the likelihood of, shall we
say, 85 per cent.

It is worthwhile perhaps dwelling a little on the functions of this
committee. They may be classified as advisory, inspectorial and
distributional.

As advisors the committee makes its estimates of what, on what it
considers to be reasonable assumptions about student numbers and
research activities, the universities will need during forthcoming
periods and presents them to the Secretary of State concerned – I
use this vague formulation intentionally since whereas in earlier
times the estimates were supposed to relate to stated quinquennia,
in recent years the response of governments at any rate has been
belated and for much shorter periods. Such estimates are not
published; and I have little doubt that the response is often
disappointing from the point of view of the committee. But there is
much to be said for a body, constituted as the committee is, being in
a position in which it is expected to make representations to
government.

As inspectors, the committee receives accounts of how its grants
have been spent and takes account of them retrospectively. It also
causes appropriate groups of its members to visit the various
universities and to listen to explanations of their problems and
ambitions. Here clearly is a method of indirect control. While as I
shall be explaining shortly, the greater part of the income grants are
not subject to restriction, evidence of the wisdom or unwisdom with
which they are spent must clearly be taken into account in
determining their magnitude for future periods. Recognition of this
fact is not brandished abroad. But it must clearly be a factor
influencing the deliberations of the governing bodies concerned.

The distributional function needs some differentiation between
grants in respect of current expenditure and grants in respect of
capital development.

The main principle inspiring the distribution of revenue is the principle of the so-called block grant. An aggregate sum is handed over without prescription as to how it is to be spent. This may be supplemented by so-called earmarked grants when considerations of public policy have led the committee to desire to foster teaching or research or both in branches of knowledge in their judgement insufficiently cultivated – the study of particular language groups for instance. But these are minor exceptions to the freedom involved by the award of block grants. In recent years, with growing numbers and particularly with recently founded universities, the size of the block grant may to some extent be conditioned by understandings regarding future intake and staffing ratios: and this is an inroad on the general principle which may well involve controversial appraisals. But it is difficult to see how it can altogether be avoided. In the main I am not prepared to cavil overmuch about such departures from the pure principle, although I am quite aware of cases where my private opinion would have been different from that of the committee.

It is in the sphere of capital grants that the functions of the committee are most delicate. Here some degree of discrimination is inevitable. Some universities have been recently founded and their opportunities for planned expansion may vary. Other universities have different needs according to the variety of research and specialisation. Not all universities can be regarded as equally eligible for expensive scientific equipment. Not all universities have graduate schools involving special library facilities. Some universities have special needs as regards the availability of residence; and so on and so forth. It is clear therefore that, when alloting capital grants, *the University Grants Committee must choose and must choose on a variety of criteria.* There is no possibility of any automatic formula of entitlement which relieves it of very difficult decisions.

On the whole, although among any assembly of vice-chancellors it would not be difficult to collect a long list of grievances in this respect, some justified, some imaginary, my impression is that, despite a growing volume of business the committee works tolerably well, and certainly very much better than any conceivable ministerial department operating according to fixed rules and liable eventually to Parliamentary questions. The main area in which I would hope for some easement of present procedures is where the marriage of governmental and other money is involved. It is obvious that this is an area where, in the absence of any rules, grave abuses might develop. But it is also obvious that undue rigidity in this respect might easily deter benefactions which would be very helpful; and it is not obvious that human ingenuity in such cases has yet reached the limits of what is possible without danger of scandal.

This brings me to the last question arising in connection with the subject of this letter, the question of ministerial responsibility. Granted that the existence of the University Grants Committee can insulate to some extent the universities in receipt of government money from the direct impact of ministerial and bureaucratic regulation, at any rate in times of reasonably good political weather, yet the committee itself must report to some ministry; and the size of its total grant and regulations regarding fees etc. must depend, in the last analysis, on Cabinet decisions and the effectiveness with which broad lines of policy in this respect are conceived and argued by ministers. The question therefore arises of what type of ministry should be involved.

As you probably know, at its inception the University Grants Committee, together with other such semi-detached buffer committees, as I think I was the first to call them, was attached to the Treasury: and I do not think that most knowledgeable persons having connections with the universities or the other bodies so connected, the Trustees of the National Gallery, the British Academy for instance, would have wished that connection to be ended. But the day came when the officials of the Treasury came to the conclusion that the monies involved had become so great, especially in regard to the universities, that the combination of the roles of game keeper and poacher could no longer be sustained. So one of the questions with which the Committee on Higher Education was confronted was what rearrangements of ministerial responsibility were advisable.

This was the one question on which our recommendations were not unanimous. The majority put forward a suggestion for a new ministry comprising responsibility for the autonomous elements in higher education, the research councils, the museums and galleries and the arts. Mr (now Sir Harold) Shearman, however, submitted a recommendation that education being, so to speak, a seamless robe, responsibility for the universities should be transferred to an enlarged Department of Education, and he alluded to the possibility of the other responsibilities discussed by the majority being thus also transferred. As you will know it was this recommendation of Sir Harold's which was in fact adopted.

Looking back on a piece of history with which I no longer feel acute personal involvement, I find it difficult now to make up my mind on the merits of the difference. I sometimes think that the majority – with which I was most intimately allied – made a mistake in confining their suggestion of a separate ministry to the so-called autonomous institutions. Much better, as I now see things, would it have been to have gone the whole hog – as in the USSR – and to have recommended a separate ministry for the whole of *higher education, autonomous or not*, plus the research bodies etc. whose inclusion we had recommended. That would have involved some administrative surgery as regards local control of the non-autonomous elements. But from the public point of view and, I now think, eventually administratively, it might have made better sense. Against this element of dubiety, I would still argue as I argued in a speech in the House of Lords (reprinted in my *University in the Modern World*) that the handling of the issues thrown up by the University Grants Committee and other buffer bodies needed – and still needs – a different administrative *style* from the handling of primary and secondary schools or perhaps indeed the junior elements of further education.

But against this, there was doubtless much cogency in Sir Harold Shearman's argument that education in the widest sense is a unity; and there was practical good sense behind the assumption that, in an already over-distended Cabinet the addition of yet another minister might have been inconvenient. And I must confess that the idea of *two* Permanent Secretaries, which was a conspicuous feature of the then government announcement of the decision to adopt one huge Department of Education and Science, never occurred to me as possible compromise between the majority and minority recommendation. I think I might have been attracted at the time. But this might also have been a mistake. Certainly, for reasons which have never been revealed, this innovation broke down at a very early stage and nothing has ever been done since to reconstitute it.

On the whole the record of the Department of Education and Science is patchy. With one exception, the Arts have been reasonably well handled by successive ministers with responsibility in their quarter and, although all such areas are liable to controversy, I would guess that the same is true of the research councils. I am bound to say that I am not so satisfied with the record of the Secretaries of State as regards the universities. They have certainly made a mess of the discriminatory fee question. So far they have quite failed to curb the influences of most universities south of the border as regards specialisation in schools. And, rightly or wrongly, some of them have managed to create in the universities themselves a feeling that they couldn't care less – which, in some circumstances, might have been salutory but can hardly be so described in the circumstances of the last few years. I am not sure that the blame is all on one side. Some academics are very quick to be sorry for themselves. But my impression is that, discounting the general effects of the financial stringency, the universities are not so happy nowadays as they were when the Chancellor of the Exchequer and his talented officials had the ultimate responsibility. Needless to say this is not to argue that there is any going back to that state of affairs.

Yours etc.

12 Higher Education: the Non-University Sector

My dear X,

Your last letter concerns an area on which so far I have only touched incidentally – the non-university sector. What were the recommendations of the Higher Education Committee in this connection? To what extent were they adopted? What do I think of the so-called binary system? And what of the position of colleges of education? These are fields in which I move with more than usual diffidence. In various ways I know the universities from inside; and although doubtless my judgements may be controversial or possibly downright wrong, they do spring from an intimate acquaintance of nearly 60 years, while I only know the other institutions from external contacts. I find the problems to which they give rise absorbingly interesting. But although I am prepared to give my ideas a run for their money, I do not put them forward with the degree of confidence born of close and prolonged experience.

Let me begin by outlining, in a very brief and superficial way, the position as it seemed to the Committee on Higher Education. As I have related, we were confronted with a massive increase in the numbers of young people who, on any just estimate, seemed to be eligible for higher education in some form or other. Some of this intake could be provided for by new universities in process of formation, some would be taken by the colleges of advanced technology, some of them institutions of long standing which, by the vision of Sir David Eccles and his able assistants, had recently been fattened up in such a way as to render them, in our judgement, as being at least as eligible as the new universities which were coming into being, for autonomous status. Below these, on the one side, was a hierarchy of technical colleges, some already preparing students for work of degree standard, others performing humbler but very essential duties of training their members in particular techniques mechanical, linguistic and commercial. On the other side were the

97

teacher-training colleges which at once provided instruction in pedagogical techniques for those who had already graduated in particular fields and, at the same time, gave more general education to aspirants to the teaching profession who had not gone to universities. There were also a certain number of more specialised institutions, some of high standing such as the College of Aeronautics at Cranfield and the Royal College of Art which presented special problems with which I do not intend to deal here.

Our recommendations in regard to this complex were briefly as follows: we recommended the planning and creation of six further universities; we recommended that a number of special institutions should be selected for rapid development in high-level teaching in sciences and technology of which Imperial College and the colleges of technology at Manchester and Glasgow should provide the nuclei; one should be developed from an existing college of advanced technology and one of the six new universities further should be planned on these lines. We recommended the upgrading of the colleges of advanced technology to the status of autonomous technological universities; we recommended the formation of a National Council for Academic Awards which should authorise the curricula for degrees of the non-autonomous technical colleges and arrange for their examinations: and we recommended some sort of federal or more intimate relationship between the teacher-training colleges and the universities.

Now for the response. Our recommendations for new universities were turned down. There were to be no new universities in England for ten years, according to then Secretary of State, although, at an early stage in our deliberations, the go-ahead had been given for one new one in Scotland – now the University of Stirling with which my own relations, as its first Chancellor watching its evolution, have been a source of much personal enlightenment and enjoyment. I don't grumble myself at this negation. Our recommendation had been based on highly misleading returns from existing, or already planned, universities regarding their future capacity. These had been very cautious; but as soon as the authorities concerned saw that expansion was accepted as the order of the day, the issue was over-subscribed, so to speak. For reasons which I will explain shortly, I regret the ten years veto. I suppose this was the response to the almost countless applications, which poured in from different localities once our recommendations were promulgated. But had we known of the willingness of the vice-chancellors to upgrade their eventual capacity, we should certainly have framed our recommendations differently.

As for the special institutions for science and technology our recommendation was turned down, on the alleged principle of not creating further hierarchical distinctions. But in fact the special fostering of Imperial College, the Manchester College of Technology and the Royal College at Glasgow – now called the University of Strathclyde – while officially repudiated on these high moral grounds, has happily taken place. One should not be upset if one's recommendations though rejected *de jure* are actually adopted *de facto*.

Our recommendations regarding the upgrading to technological universities of the colleges of advance technology were adopted. This was gratifying in itself and thoroughly well deserved. But it had a further significance, less consistent with the vision of the future as promulgated by a subsequent Secretary of State for Education whose plans I will discuss in detail shortly.

But first a word about our conception of the increase of universities in general. Here, as in the case of the upgrading of the colleges of advanced technology, we considered building to some extent on established foundations. We hoped that some of the regional colleges, central institutions and colleges of education (as it was proposed renaming the teacher-training colleges) could gradually be given university status – the status that is to say of quasi-autonomous corporations coming under the University Grants Committee, rather than directly under local or central authority. In this sense we hoped that there would be preserved so to speak a more or less continuous spectrum in the developing system of higher education. Our recommendation of the creation of the National Council for Academic Awards was designed to be part of such a continuous system.

But in this respect we reckoned without a later Secretary of State, Mr Anthony Crosland, one of the most amiable and thoughtful members of the Labour Government of the middle 1960s. In his famous speech of 27 April 1965 at the Woolwich Polytechnic, he definitely rejected our conception of a *unitary* system in the sense in which I have presented it and substituted for it the conception of a *binary* or dual system in which, on the one side, there should be the university sector making what he described as 'its own unique and marvellous contribution' in which he 'of course' now included the colleges of advanced technology; and, on the other, the public sector headed by polytechnics, existing or to be created, of which he praised Woolwich as a leading example, with greatly expanded teacher-training colleges and the various other technical colleges keeping up the rear with the National Council for Academic Awards as the guardian of degree giving standards. He went out of the way to compare his conception with the Grandes Ecoles in France, the Technische Hochschulen in Germany, the Zurich Tech, and the Leningrad Poly in the Soviet Union. This speech was of such momentous significance for the development of our higher education system, that you will pardon me if I subject it to somewhat extended critical comment. I spoke against it at the time in a speech in the House of Lords of 1 December 1965 (reprinted in my *University in the Modern World*, pp. 138–57). But my appraisal here will follow somewhat different, although not contradictory, lines.

The first reflection which occurs to me, rereading Mr Crosland's speech after so many years, is the quite amazing comparison with what he could legitimately hope to do with the polytechnics, with the status of the *Grandes Ecoles* and the continental *Technische Hochschulen*. The *Grandes Ecoles* have long had an eminence vastly superior to the ordinary French universities. So too is the relationship of the *Zurich Tech* to its Swiss cantonally supported universities. As for the German Technological *Hochschulen*, whatever may have been their beginnings, their contemporary ranking must surely be with our own Imperial College or Strathclyde rather than with the polytechnics.

This brings me to my second reflection. If the object of the exercise was to raise the standing of the public sector to equal and healthy parity with the university sector, was it not an unfortunate thing, from the Crosland point of view, that the colleges of advanced technology were to be included in the university sector? Surely this was a case of locking the door of the stable when the horse had bolted. The colleges of advanced technology had been fattened up to university standards, and, in a logically conceived public sector, should have been the leading contributor to 'mutual understanding and healthy rivalry' to use Mr Crosland's own words – where the systems overlapped.

This in turn leads to a further perplexity. The burden of part at least of Mr Crosland's recommendation was the necessity for 'vocationally orientated' institutions. But as Lord Ashby has shown, the technologies had already established themselves in the university sector in spite of some opposition; and if medicine and law and engineering are not vocationally orientated, it would be difficult to say what is. The supreme examples in this country – the parallels to the Grandes Ecoles and Zurich Tech, and the other famous continental Hochschulen – where are they to be found, if not in Imperial College, the Manchester College of Technology, and Strathclyde?

For all these reasons and more which might be mentioned, I cannot help thinking that Mr Crosland's vision of the justification of what he conceived as the 'Public Sector', at any rate of the functions of the polytechnics, was more than a trifle confused. And since the rulings, based on this vision and promulgated at Woolwich, definitely created barriers between the public sector and the university sector which had not been so definite before – no more universities for ten years, colleges of education to keep their existing status and affiliation – barriers which, on our conception of the spectrum, might have been sensibly diminished, I cannot help feeling that, with the best will in the world, Mr Crosland was taking premature and regrettable decisions.

I personally think that a better case can be made for some of these decisions than the arguments by which they were supported. I hasten to say that I don't think this case should have been *decisive*. But at all events, it would have presented its opponents with arguments which were more difficult to criticise. Supposing that it could be established that the majority of English, as distinct from Scottish universities were themselves on the wrong track; that the tendency of these, more or less autonomous institutions to a premature specialisation at the undergraduate stage and their forcing the unsuitable dropping of what many would consider more or less essential subjects at the later stages of schooling was irrevocable. Would this not have been some valid pretext for providing alternative training at a high level in the public sector. Might we not imagine Mr Crosland saying to himself 'Most, though not all, of the universities South of the Border are pretty hopeless. They are alright at producing aces who will go on to be themselves university teachers or successful competitors in the examination for the administrative grade of the public service – though some of them look down their noses quite gratuitously at the American habit of reserving such specialisation for the graduate school. But, from the point of view of many students of average second-class ability, who are many more than the aces, much of this is irrelevant and boring.

A broader education, such as prevails in the Scottish universities and the rest of the English speaking world, is much more suitable for promoting versatility and general culture. I can't interfere with the freedom of the universities; it is intrinsically contrary to my principles. But I can at least promote institutions in the public sector, not ignoring the vocational element on training but backing it up, in the mode recommended by Ashby, with wider cultural and general interests. The colleges of advanced technology would have been the best medium for this. But there are regional technical colleges, straining at the leash to acquire superior status, which can still provide something of what I want.'

As I have indicated this, in my judgement, would have been a second best. The better alternative would have been a change of policy on the part of the English universities, not abruptly dropping all specialisation in first degrees – the Scottish universities and the best American establishments do not do that – but broadening the fundamental basis and transferring intense specialisation to graduate schools, in which many of them have a long way to go before they rival what happens in at least a dozen American universities, refraining from and spoiling the later stages of school education. They could have done this if they had the will; and having the existing talent already, it would have not involved perhaps so many years of confusion before many of the proposed polytechnics got things right.

But matters have happened another way. The polytechnics are here; and by a queer accident of the recently prevalent incomes policies, they have derived an unexpected advantage over the universities as regards the financial attractions they can offer for the recruitment of most grades of staff – an accident, which I must say, involved much injustice to the universities and great, and very well deserved, discredit to the minister responsible. But in spite of many teething troubles – Mr Crosland was deceiving himself if he thought you could easily produce efficient and harmonious higher educational bodies by steam-rollering together geographically non-contiguous and intellectually disparate institutions – highly interesting experiments are going on. I doubt if he will ever get his Grandes Ecoles or Zurich Tech in this sector. But men of goodwill in the English universities should give their competitors sympathetic understanding and wish them good luck in trying to do something which they might have done themselves, had they, other than at Oxford and a few other places not having phobias for mixed degrees and diplomas, shown the slightest inclination to attempt to do so.

Perhaps some day the polytechnics will be permitted to call themselves universities – though it is to be hoped that, in that event, they will not try to remodel their curricula on those of so many of their fellows South of the Border.

As for the further decision arising from the Secretary of State's binary philosophy – the retention of the colleges of education under the administrative and financial control of their present sponsors, this was a real disappointment. The suggestion that they should be federated with suitable universities arose originally in the McNair report; and its elaboration which, it is an open secret, was conceived by that great academic administrator Sir Philip Morris, was thought by all concerned to be one of our really good ideas. I personally thought that it would be good for the colleges as fostering their feeling of status which many of them felt – rightly as I conceived things – to be that of the Cinderella of the higher education system; and good for the universities as forcing them into taking more seriously arrangements for broad-based degrees. And the proposal received the support of men much better fitted than I was to decide on its advisability. The late Lord Silkin and Lord Eccles, with their vast experience of educational administration, both spoke in its favour in a debate in the Second Chamber.

But it was not to be. Partly I think the rejection sprang from Mr Crosland's fixation on the binary system: this certainly appears from the phraseology of the Woolwich speech, although by that time the universities had indicated their willingness to venture on this experiment. But partly there was perhaps a more practical reason. At the time of our report there was a pronounced shortage of teachers; and the officials of the Department, not unnaturally, wished to avoid any interruption to the main job of the colleges, the production of many more. This motive suggested itself from the wording of an early promulgation of policy in which the words 'for the present' indicated the possibility that the decision not to adopt our policy might be mitigated later on.

Whether this was so or not, it cannot be said that the colleges have been particularly fortunate in their subsequent history. There was a fascinating inquiry by a committee under Lord James which released a whole sheaf of possible changes in curricula, length of courses and requirements for degrees of various kinds. But for the most part these have remained in the air: and meantime the shortage of teachers has been overtaken by a changed demographic situation which surely should have been foreseen earlier; and a good many of the present population of the colleges are wondering where they will get jobs.

I cannot help feeling therefore that our suggestion that the colleges might be integrated in the university system with mutual benefits to all concerned is still relevant. But this is a matter for the future of higher education which I know you wish me to discuss at greater length.

Yours etc.

13 Higher Education and the Future

My dear X,

I am sure you do not want this correspondence to go on for ever. But it has involved various questions and criticisms which bear not only on the past but also on the future; and I feel that it is up to me to say something about my hopes and fears in this respect before bringing it to a conclusion.

Fortunately my task in this connection has been considerably simplified by the issue from the Department of Education and Science, together with the Scottish Education Department, of a discussion paper entitled 'Higher Education into the 1990s'. This document is one of the best written and most thought-provoking in my experience ever to have issued from Whitehall whose publications, although written by some of the most intelligent men in the country, are usually so smeared over by reservations and evasions, inserted by, or anticipating the desires of ministers, as to be both elusive and highly unreadable. This one, however, is clear and straightforward; it sets forth various possibilities and the implications which they involve, with a concision and candour which can have few precedents in this kind of publication.

The occasion for this paper is the realisation that the fall in the birth rate since 1964 must mean a contraction in the eighteen-year-old population by 1982–3 falling much more steeply from 1990–1 onwards: the numbers are already born and can only be affected by further changes in the relevant number of deaths or migration. It then sets forth three alternative hypotheses regarding the number of these and others who may be anticipated to participate, with unchanged policies, in higher education, both full-time and sandwich courses, and reveals that the population concerned may be assumed to increase in various degrees in the 1980s, and then in the early 1990s plunge downward, on the lowest hypotheses *below* the level of 1976, on the middle that of 1980–1 and on the highest that of 1984–5.

The lowest hypothesis does not present much of a problem with an increase from 1976–7 of some 30,000 in 1984–5, with a decline by roughly the same figure in 1990. But both the middle and high hypotheses show quite substantial increases and eventual declines: the middle some 80,000 by 1986–7, declining thereafter to a little above the original figure in 1994–5; and the highest to over 160,000 in 1989–90 declining by more than 60,000 by 1994–5. Clearly the possibility of bulges of this kind must raise all sorts of difficulties which the paper proceeds to discuss with the aid of various models.

I will not follow this procedure here since my object is, not so much to endorse one or other of the alternatives or some combination of features of several, as to indicate the bearing of various points which I have tried to make in the course of our exchange on the desirable conditions of an eventual solution.

Let me say at once that I still believe in the so-called 'Robbins' principle – a complete misnomer since it was the unanimous recommendation of a whole committee – namely that places in higher education should be available for all those who have the ability and willingness to benefit by them. To go back on this would be to go back on the fundamental principle of equality of opportunity in so far as that does not involve the break-up of the family and its inherent advantages. It would involve denying to persons who would have satisfied these criteria nowadays the same opportunities in the future. It would involve raising the already very exacting conditions of testing the degree of ability involved.

But, at the same time, I would insist on the condition which was coupled with this principle, namely that so far as places in the universities are involved there should be adequate facilities for studies in breadth as well as in depth. And it is very clear to me that so far as many universities in England – not Scotland – are concerned this will entail quite a considerable change in present arrangements. Let me list these in their main outlines.

First they would entail the elimination of most special requirements in A levels, or whatever may take the place of the advanced school leaving examination in future. The iniquitous habit, not universal, of ultra-specialisation at tender ages would have to go. Whether they like it or not, all but the most exceptional pupils in the most exceptional subjects would have to continue, as they do elsewhere, with a broad spread of the basic subjects of a civilised equipment: English, mathematics, natural science, history, geography and two languages other than their own; and while uniform excellence in each would not (repeat *not*) be required, a reasonable average would.

Secondly, while in the first degree, a complete *à la carte* choice would not be available, there would be alternative *Table d'hôte* courses, at any rate in Part I. The same should be available for Part II for those who preferred to proceed on the same plane of generality. At the same time, for those who preferred to narrow their focus, there should be a suitable spread of central and related auxiliary subjects. Equally important, the arrangements for supervision should not be such as to lead those who chose the more general degree courses to feel that they were less well looked after than those who chose some degree of specialisation.

Thirdly, extreme specialisation suitable for preparation for high research scholarship or professional training should be reserved for the graduate schools in respect of which the admission requirements, while preserving some degree of flexibility, should certainly not be automatic and should be subject to strict conditions as regards earlier performance.

These conditions would certainly make many academic boards south of the border blanche with terror or indignation. But they are conditions which prevail over the greater part of the rest of the English speaking world – Scotland, Canada, most of the US universities, South Africa, Australia, New Zealand. And in my view we have simply got to realise that, as regards specialisation at the later stages of schooling, we are completely out of step with the rest of the free societies – including Scotland; and run the acute danger of turning out a race of citizens virtually uncomprehending each other as regards the broader topics of civilised talk and equally of being incapable of conveying thought in our own language to many of the inhabitants of other great Western language areas, save in staccato instructions to waiters and taxi-drivers. If we could get rid of this disability perhaps we could tolerate rather more specialisation in first degrees than seems ideal, although considerably less than prevails at present in many subjects, conspiciously my own – economics, whose contemporary practitioners should realise more than they seem to do at present the importance of the dictum – was it John Stuart Mill's? – that an economist who is only an economist, unless he is a genius (to whom none of these strictures applies) is not much use even as an economist, in most walks of life in respect of most practical questions.

But what would happen to numbers under the so-called

'Robbins' principle, thus interpreted – as it was from the first by its promulgators?

I frankly don't know. Some school children who are only interested in one subject, either because they are congenitally that way or because the other subjects are poorly taught, might be deterred from pursuing a more all-round course up to the school-leaving age and thus might flinch from the thought of some mixture in Part I of the first degree. But I doubt if thoughtful parents would take conformity with schooling systems in most other countries that way; and while sudden change without sufficient notice – which I don't recommend – is always disturbing, I don't think the effect on numbers of readjustment of the A level requirements and the preliminary preparation would have much adverse effect and, in the end, might be favourable.

As regards other changes recommended in these letters, the Prest system of loans, repayable only in the event of pecuniary success, might make some parents apprehensive, if it were not properly explained. Even if it were, the disappearance of something for nothing at other people's expense in favour of something for moderate repayment provisions, if and when income permits, might result in some limitation of applications. It is certainly a possibility. But if it took place for these reasons, although I should adhere to the compelling reasons of distributive justice which I have set forth earlier, I should regret it.

Matters would be different if my other suggestion for most people, in between the limits represented by Mozart and Einstein, of a period between school leaving before loans (à la Prest) or grants were available, should result in a reduction of applicants. In that event I should not be depressed at all. As I have argued earlier, it is not an intrinsically bad thing for a young person to have had some experience of the ordinary business of life at humble levels, before deciding whether or not to try to come full time to an institution of higher education. The doubts which one has about the motivation of a margin of the present population of students would be resolved. The students would have learnt by inquiry what to expect and the teachers would know what was expected of them in dealing with persons with more adult experience.

On balance, I would hope that the intensification of secondary education and the general spread of knowledge concerning the superior advantages for those with the ability, would sustain the growth in participation rates, so that even when the population bulge of the early 1980s had begun to decline, notwithstanding the restraining factors I have mentioned, there would still be a tendency to an upward trend in numbers in higher education. After all we must recognise that there is still some leeway to make up as regards women students: and, for reasons adequately set forth by Moser and Layard in the appendices to the Report on Higher Education and subsequent publications, I would think that there were still untapped resources of worthwhile talent in the families of manual workers. I am not ignorant of the hypothesis of capillary tendencies in the ability composition of the population and am not prepared to discuss it as totally without foundation – though I certainly think it is usually used to sustain attitudes of which I disapprove morally. But I certainly believe that the gap between recruitment from large families in such income groups and small ones is not to be explained by genetic factors: and I am afraid that some at least of the different advantage taken of existing facilities for higher education between the upper as compared with the lower income groups is to be explained by tradition and ignorance as much as by inborn qualities, ridiculous as it may be to deny all genetic and family influences. Hence I should not worry too much about the long-term trend in the 1990s. Clearly declines further than at present anticipated, in the size of the average family might create new difficulties. But against this must be put the strong possibility that by that time there will be a considerably greater demand for post-experience courses for people of mature years. This is already beginning to make itself felt; and I will expatiate on it later.

Nevertheless the problem of what to do about the bulge of the early 1980s remains. Clearly on the centre and higher assumption of the Department of Education projections this involves some difficulties. Some of these might be solved by introducing the kind of deferment of grants or loans I have suggested. But I doubt whether these would eliminate some bulge.

Here the problems will lie partly in the realm of buildings, partly in the realm of manpower.

So far as buildings are concerned I do not think the problem is too difficult. Some institutions of higher education are inadequately housed owing to the cuts of the last few years. I don't share the euphoria of ministers and their opponents that our financial difficulties will necessarily be solved by the presence in office of either group – I would only be more sanguine if I saw emerging some non-partisan, non-vote seeking agreement between moderate men and women of the centre. But I don't see why some building should not go on. And I see no objection whatever to the suggestion in the White Paper that some buildings and residences could be hired for what temporary needs may be left.

The position as regards staff is different; and my views in this connection would certainly be repudiated by most academics in the United Kingdom. But this reflection does not lead me to reject them. Indeed when I hear friends predicting 'disaster', catastrophe and so on from the impact of recent financial limitations – which needless to say I regret – I feel impelled to tell them not to repeat their complaints outside to educationalists in most other parts of the world; otherwise they will be greeted with mild mirth or even unseemly shouts of laughter. A university system with an average staff/student ratio of, even now, less than 1 : 10 is not going to be 'shattered' by the movement of a few adverse points in that ratio. While I certainly would be extremely sorry to see the very much greater adverse ratios prevailing in some Western countries, I personally have seen, prevailing in some institutions in this country in the past, staff/student ratios of up to, say, 1 : 15 while the departments concerned were achieving high standards of inter-national excellence.

Therefore if the bulge involves some pressure on prevailing staff/student ratios, I do not think it will mean the end of the world – although I would not wish to be underestimating the difficulties of vice-chancellors and others in the inevitable depart-mental and interdepartmental adjustments. The implications would be that rather more attention than is usual should be paid to the organisation of courses of studies, and somewhat harder work on the part of staff and students. As a spectator, I should not regard this with positive relish. But I don't think it would be intolerable; and I don't think that standards of teaching need suffer – there is a very considerable slack for improvement and economy in this connec-tion. As for research, while there is an inner core which should be maintained at all costs, I cannot believe that there is not a margin which is undertaken largely for the promotional purposes which I have discussed in an earlier letter. There is probably more research of one kind or another going on in this country at present, than has taken place through all previous history. It is really difficult to believe that the degree of compression imposed by the prospective bulge and some (small) adjustment of the staff/student ratio would create problems which deserve the doleful adjectives sometimes applied to them. The main trouble I should fear in this connection would be that some completely first-class people, oppressed by comparatively low incomes and high taxation, should be lured abroad by offers of more tempting positions. But that trouble springs from general government policy in this country and, in present circumstances, would exist even if there were no prospective bulge. Successive Cabinets of both Parties have looked after that. We certainly should not find any likely increase in the higher education population very difficult to deal with if our general rate of economic growth had been of the order of magnitude of that of Germany or Japan in the last 20 years.

Later on, if the financial position does not worsen – which is not at all out of the question – I do not think that the predicted decline in the future demand for higher education need cause excessive apprehension. Even on the lowest assumptions concerning the eventual size of the average family and the consequential demand for educational facilities immediately, or shortly after, leaving school, I suspect that there will arise a considerably extended demand for renewal of education at a later age. The success of the Open University, about which so many academics were so sceptical, has revealed that there are already large numbers of persons of mature years who wish to take the degrees which they might have taken at an earlier stage. I can easily conceive that there may exist an even larger potential of persons who already have gone through the normal processes of higher education who would wish, if suitable facilities were available, to renew their contacts with the progress which has been made with subjects which they have already taken, or even to extend their knowledge in other fields. Knowledge becomes ever more extensive; and, if one is not to fall behind the explanation of some aspects of its complications, access from time to time, to suitably arranged courses is not only professionally more and more desirable, but also from wider points of view enjoyable and spiritually renewing.

Let it not be claimed that this is a novel proposal. Post-experience courses exist already in some institutions of higher education in this country; they ought to exist much more in the Colleges of Education. In other parts of the world, particularly the USA, they begin to flourish. I would claim, however, that from the glimpse of such developments on a much larger scale than at present exists in this country and which appear in the Department of Education discussion paper, that this is one of the most imaginative and forward-looking proposals ever to issue from official quarters in Whitehall; and I do think their adoption would be good in itself and might materially ease the problems of future demographic trends.

I would like to emphasise, however, that developments of this sort would need careful preparation and arrangements quite different from those suitable for those which are appropriate to the organisation of first degrees or the normal procedures of graduate schools. Persons of mature years who would enjoy and benefit from post-experience courses of various kinds, obviously cannot absent themselves from their normal occupations for periods comparable to those required by present arrangements in full-time first, or subsequent, degrees. They will also have arrived at stages in their lives at which, for many of them, the testing of benefits received by examinations of the normal type will often be wholly inappropriate. How many middle-aged professors would survive the ordeal of the examinations they set and organise? The desirable methods of instruction will also be different – and so perhaps will the demands on the intuition of the teachers. Nevertheless, I suspect that there is enough talent available today in various existing institutions of higher education, with suitable encouragement, to make extensive developments of this sort intrinsically worthwhile and vastly beneficial to the efficiency and spiritual solidarity of the community.

I could continue to expatiate further. But this correspondence must have its limits. . . .

As you will have gathered throughout, I am not of the complacent view that higher education in this country is not confronted with very difficult problems, problems of organisation, discipline, focus and adjustment: I do not respond sympathetically when I hear ministers and academics claiming that ours is the best higher educational system in the world. I can easily think of comparisons of aspects in which we are obviously surpassed, just as I can equally think of aspects in which we probably excel; this kind of vapid post-prandial generalisation is not profitable. But I would say – and this is my concluding thought – that, in spite of many things which need to be put right and with all our imperfections, there is still scope in the system to afford to any serious-minded man or woman who feels so disposed, absorbing and inspiring careers both in the teaching of the young and the not so young, and in furthering the advancement of knowledge. Indeed when I reflect on the ambiguous prospects of our contemporary British society, with all its perilous external insecurity and its internal contradictions of groups and of purpose, I should be inclined to argue that one of the main hopes of improvement in the future lies in what can be, and sometimes is, fostered by the institutions of higher education.

Yours etc.

Index